AngularJS Deployment Essentials

Learn how to optimally deploy your AngularJS applications to today's top hosting environments

Zachariah Moreno

BIRMINGHAM - MUMBAI

AngularJS Deployment Essentials

First published: February 2015

Production reference: 1250215

Published by Packt Publishing Ltd.
Livery Place
35 Livery Street
Birmingham B3 2PB, UK.

ISBN 978-1-78398-358-2

www.packtpub.com

Credits

Author
Zachariah Moreno

Reviewers
Kent C. Dodds
Ladislav Gažo
K. Aava Rani

Commissioning Editor
Andrew Duckworth

Acquisition Editors
Richard Harvey
James Jones

Content Development Editor
Adrian Raposo

Technical Editors
Ruchi Desai
Rosmy George

Copy Editors
Rashmi Sawant
Ashwati Thampi

Project Coordinator
Kinjal Bari

Proofreaders
Maria Gould
Paul Hindle
Chris Smith

Indexer
Rekha Nair

Graphics
Disha Haria
Abhinash Sahu

Production Coordinator
Nilesh R. Mohite

Cover Work
Nilesh R. Mohite

About the Author

Zachariah Moreno is a 23-year-old web developer from Sacramento, California, who works for the state government and enjoys contributing to open source projects of the web variety. Zach completed an internship with Google in 2012 and graduated with his BS in web development from the Art Institute of California—Sacramento, in the following year. He has published an article entitled *AngularJS Tool Stack* in Software Developer's Journal. Zach can typically be found on Google+ discussing design, developer tools, workflow, camping, golf, and his English bulldog, Gladstone.

About the Reviewers

Kent C. Dodds is a frontend software engineer at Alianza, Inc. He's actively involved in the frontend community on Twitter (`@kentcdodds`) and through his various projects on GitHub (`kentcdodds`). He is a cohost to Angular Air, a live video podcast all about AngularJS. He is also an instructor at Egghead.io (`https://egghead.io/`), a site dedicated to bite-sized videos teaching web development skills. He spends most of his free time with his wife and two kids or coding.

> I would like to thank Domo Technologies for getting me started on frontend web development as well as Angular. I would like to thank my wife, Brooke, for her patience while I worked on this book, and all the other projects that have occupied my time.

Ladislav Gažo is a long-time computer enthusiast and has been digging into the software world since his youth. He has more than 12 years of professional experience in development and software engineering. While starting experiments with computer graphics and network administration, he realized the true path is toward the combination of software engineering and business. He has been developing, analyzing, and architecting Java-based, desktop-based, and finally, modern web-based solutions for several years. The application of the Agile approach and advanced technology is both his hobby and daily job.

Rich experience with various technologies led him to cofound Seges, a software development company in Slovakia. He actively participates in start-up events and helps build development communities, namely Google Developer Group and Java Group, in Slovakia. With his colleagues, he designed and spun off an interactive content management solution called Synapso, utilizing contemporary technologies combined with user experience in mind.

He has also worked on the books *Learning Apache Karaf*, *Apache Karaf Cookbook*, and *Learning Karaf Cellar*, all by Packt Publishing.

> I would not have been able to realize my knowledge as part of the review process of this book without the support of all my colleagues, friends, and family. Creating a good long-term environment helped me gain the experience that I can pass further on.

K. Aava Rani is a cofounder of CulpzLab Pvt Ltd, a software company with 10 years of experience in game technologies. A successful blogger and technologist, she switched her focus to game development in 2004. Since then, she has produced a number of game titles and has provided art and programming solutions to Unity developers across the globe. She is based in New Delhi, India. She has been the recipient of several prestigious awards, including Adobe for Game Technology Expert 2012 and SmartFoxServer, for her articles. She has experience in various different technologies.

Aava is cofounder of CulpzLab, a software development company of highly skilled professionals in web game development and interactive media. Founded in 2010, CulpzLab has proven itself to be a reliable technology partner for its clients. Currently, CulpzLab employs over 50 people and has its office based out of New Delhi, India.

CulpzLab is a leading-edge custom (bespoke) process-driven software solutions provider that has helped and partnered with many reputable brands, start-up ventures, and offshore IT companies. It has helped them realize and deliver effective, efficient, and on-time digital solutions.

CulpzLab has worked globally with a plethora of clients with a diverse technology background, industry expertise, and a client footprint that extends to more than 14 countries. CulpzLab is well positioned to help organizations derive maximum value from their IT investments and fully support their business aims.

CulpzLab's core business purpose is to invent, engineer, and deliver technology solutions that drive business value, create social value, and improve the lives of customers.

She has also worked on *Creating E-learning Games with Unity3D, Packt Publishing*.

I would like to acknowledge the creators of the Unity3D program, an amazing tool that allows the ultimate digital experience in creative expression. I'd also like to thank my clients for being part of the fun! Many of you have become good friends through my creative successes. Finally, I'd like to thank R. K. Rajanjan who taught me how to love technologies.

www.PacktPub.com

Support files, eBooks, discount offers, and more

For support files and downloads related to your book, please visit www.PacktPub.com.

Did you know that Packt offers eBook versions of every book published, with PDF and ePub files available? You can upgrade to the eBook version at www.PacktPub.com and as a print book customer, you are entitled to a discount on the eBook copy. Get in touch with us at service@packtpub.com for more details.

At www.PacktPub.com, you can also read a collection of free technical articles, sign up for a range of free newsletters and receive exclusive discounts and offers on Packt books and eBooks.

https://www2.packtpub.com/books/subscription/packtlib

Do you need instant solutions to your IT questions? PacktLib is Packt's online digital book library. Here, you can search, access, and read Packt's entire library of books.

Why subscribe?

- Fully searchable across every book published by Packt
- Copy and paste, print, and bookmark content
- On demand and accessible via a web browser

Free access for Packt account holders

If you have an account with Packt at www.PacktPub.com, you can use this to access PacktLib today and view 9 entirely free books. Simply use your login credentials for immediate access.

Table of Contents

Preface

Where is AngularJS? Since AngularJS's inception, it has been deployed into a multitude of different environments, mostly due to its flexibility and extensibility. Parallel to Angular's rise are developer tools such as Apache Cordova and Chrome packaged apps. These have given developers the opportunity to deploy web applications on platforms that were previously dominated by languages such as Java and C. With these advancements, AngularJS apps can now be found in the Chrome Web Store, Google Play Store, Apple App Store, PlayStation Store, and Firefox Marketplace, all in addition to traditional in-browser web applications. To see examples of other members of the AngularJS community that are built on AngularJS, `https://builtwith.angularjs.org/` is a phenomenal place. As AngularJS and its community mature, I suspect that the aforementioned question will become "Where isn't AngularJS?"

Without a talented and thriving developer community, AngularJS would not be the framework that it is today. The most apparent metric I found to measure this phenomenon is the rate at which the new versions of AngularJS are released. At its apex, it reaches 3 minor releases in 1 day and 5 minor releases per month in March 2014. To help the community and contributors keep up with the pace of development, the AngularJS core team maintains the website `https://dashboard.angularjs.org/`, which provides a real-time snapshot into the current build status of AngularJS's core. Because of its extensible design, contributors have also been able to enhance AngularJS's core through the development of third-party modules, services, filters, and directives. Some examples are the popular REST Angular module for consuming RESTful APIs, the Angular-UI frontend framework, Ionic Framework for mobile UIs, Firebase real-time data storage and syncing, and Yoeman generators for Angular.

What this book covers

Chapter 1, Our App and Tool Stack, explains the tooling process, which is one of the hottest topics in today's web development community, and AngularJS has a suite of tools that enhances your developer experience. You will learn about Angular's tool stack, how they fit together, and most notably, how they can help you deploy and maintain future applications.

Chapter 2, Deploying to Apache, explains why Apache, being the most popular web server environment, is a solid platform for hosting most Angular applications. You will get an opportunity to enhance Apache's default configuration to best support your Angular application. We will also discuss best practices to determine whether Apache is suitable for your type of application or whether an alternate infrastructure should be considered.

Chapter 3, Deploying to Heroku, discusses Heroku, which is one of the best platforms as a service. Its infrastructure empowers developers to spin up, deploy to, and scale their own Node.js servers at a minimal cost. Deploying to Heroku is a positive developer experience because its tool speed and efficiency are second to none.

Chapter 4, Deploying to Firebase Hosting, explains why Firebase has only been offering PaaS for a few months, but the promise of hosting your application code in the same environment as your real-time database has created a lot of interest around the Firebase services. You will learn how Firebase is preconfigured to optimally serve the AngularJS applications and how to further tailor Firebase Hosting to your application's needs.

Chapter 5, Deploying a Mobile App, explains why hybrid mobile apps is not a new idea, but the quality and tooling around it has made it a strong contender when building a mobile application. We will take our application's code and build it for Android/iOS using PhoneGap, Apache Cordova, and Cordova Chrome Apps.

Chapter 6, Deploying as Chrome Apps, explains why Chrome OS's adoption is growing at an exponential rate and the need for developers to support this platform is parallel in importance. Angular thrives in this environment, and deploying our application as a Chrome App for consumption on the Chrome Web Store/Chrome OS is an exciting frontier for both developers and consumers.

Chapter 7, Postdeployment, explains why deployment is no exception to the marketing adage of "rinse, lather, repeat", because it is never finished. Optimizing your workflow with best practices is necessary to ensure the longevity of your application. We will enhance our application and grok how to safely deploy the enhancement into production.

Chapter 8, Conclusion – AngularJS Deployment Essentials, explains that harnessing the tools will allow you to deploy a single AngularJS application to new platforms and new customers. We will discuss a few tips that will help you get the best out of these tools.

What you need for this book

The materials needed for this book include the, somewhat obvious, tools typically associated with most forms of web development. This includes a computer with the operating system of your choice, a stable Internet connection, an application to create and edit text files, basic working knowledge of your computer's command line, an instance of each modern web browser, and because it is paramount to stay hydrated while groking new information, water. All other software and tools needed to accomplish the examples in this book are covered in *Chapter 1, Our App and Tool Stack*.

Who this book is for

This book is designed to build your existing knowledge of AngularJS development with the tools and best practices necessary to successfully deploy an application into a stable production environment. Thus, prior understanding of HTML, CSS, JavaScript, the MV* architecture, and AngularJS are needed by you to fully implement the techniques and best practices covered in this book. If you have committed to this book and aren't feeling confident about the antecedent criterion, the AngularJS community has published a surfeit of free resources (listed as follows) that will adequately prepare you to assimilate the knowledge to come:

- `http://egghead.io`
- `http://thinkster.io`
- `https://github.com/jmcunningham/AngularJS-Learning`

Conventions

In this book, you will find a number of styles of text that distinguish between different kinds of information. Here are some examples of these styles, and an explanation of their meaning.

Code words in text are shown as follows: "This file is called `manifest.json`."

A block of code is set as follows:

```
angular.module('krakn.controllers', ['ionic', 'ngAnimate'])
.controller('HomeCtrl', ['$scope', 'syncData', function($scope,
  syncData) {
  syncData('syncedValue').$bind($scope, 'syncedValue');
}]);
```

When we wish to draw your attention to a particular part of a code block, the relevant lines or items are set in bold:

```
angular.module('krakn.controllers', ['ionic', 'ngAnimate'])
.controller('HomeCtrl', ['$scope', 'syncData', function($scope,
  syncData) {
  syncData('syncedValue').$bind($scope, 'syncedValue');
}]);
```

New terms and **important words** are shown in bold. Words that you see on the screen, in menus or dialog boxes for example, appear in the text like this: "From the drop-down menu, select the **Settings** menu item near the bottom."

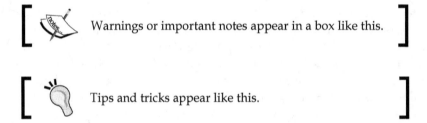

Warnings or important notes appear in a box like this.

Tips and tricks appear like this.

From this point forward, I will use a few terms I consider to be relevant industry standard slang and acronyms to enhance your vocabulary when speaking with other developers, watching tutorial videos online, and reading associated literature or blog posts. These include the following terms:

- **Angular**: This term is a shorthand name referring to all facets of AngularJS and its community.

- **Tool Stack**: This term is used for a collection of tools encompassing all phases of the development process. These include, but are not limited to, boilerplates/seed projects, code editors, IDEs, code linters, command-line utilities, language abstraction compilers, package managers, local web servers, LiveReload, source/version control and their respective web applications, web browsers / BrowserStack, browser DevTools, testing runners, build tools, server communication clients, and others. For further information, Google search for slides from Paul Irish's presentation entitled *Tooling & The Webapp Development Stack*.

- **DevTools**: This term is a shorthand name referring to the Google Chrome Developer Tools. Having contributed to the Chromium Open Source community, I am biased towards Google Chrome and most notably towards the Chrome Developer Tools.

- **PaaS**: This term is an acronym for Platform as a Service.

- **CLI**: This term is an acronym for command-line interface.

Reader feedback

Feedback from our readers is always welcome. Let us know what you think about this book—what you liked or disliked. Reader feedback is important for us as it helps us develop titles that you will really get the most out of.

To send us general feedback, simply e-mail `feedback@packtpub.com`, and mention the book's title in the subject of your message.

If there is a topic that you have expertise in and you are interested in either writing or contributing to a book, see our author guide at `www.packtpub.com/authors`.

Customer support

Now that you are the proud owner of a Packt book, we have a number of things to help you to get the most from your purchase.

Errata

Although we have taken every care to ensure the accuracy of our content, mistakes do happen. If you find a mistake in one of our books—maybe a mistake in the text or the code—we would be grateful if you could report this to us. By doing so, you can save other readers from frustration and help us improve subsequent versions of this book. If you find any errata, please report them by visiting `http://www.packtpub.com/submit-errata`, selecting your book, clicking on the **Errata Submission Form** link, and entering the details of your errata. Once your errata are verified, your submission will be accepted and the errata will be uploaded to our website or added to any list of existing errata under the Errata section of that title.

To view the previously submitted errata, go to `https://www.packtpub.com/books/content/support` and enter the name of the book in the search field. The required information will appear under the **Errata** section.

Piracy

Piracy of copyrighted material on the Internet is an ongoing problem across all media. At Packt, we take the protection of our copyright and licenses very seriously. If you come across any illegal copies of our works in any form on the Internet, please provide us with the location address or website name immediately so that we can pursue a remedy.

Please contact us at copyright@packtpub.com with a link to the suspected pirated material.

We appreciate your help in protecting our authors and our ability to bring you valuable content.

Questions

If you have a problem with any aspect of this book, you can contact us at questions@packtpub.com, and we will do our best to address the problem.

1
Our App and Tool Stack

Before NASA or Space X launches a vessel into the cosmos, there is a tremendous amount of planning and preparation involved. The guiding principle when planning for any successful mission is similar to minimizing efforts and resources while retaining maximum return on the mission. Our principles for development and deployment are no exception to this axiom, and you will gain a firmer working knowledge of how to do so in this chapter.

In this chapter, you will learn how to do the following:

- Minimize efforts and maximize results using a tool stack optimized for AngularJS development
- Access the krakn app via GitHub for deployment in future chapters
- Scaffold an Angular app with Yeoman, Grunt, and Bower
- Set up a local Node.js development server
- Read through krakn's source code

The right tools for the job

Web applications can be compared to buildings; without tools, neither would be a pleasure to build. This makes tools an indispensable factor in both development and construction. When tools are combined, they form a workflow that can be repeated across any project built with the same stack, facilitating the practices of design, development, and deployment. The argument can be made that it is just as paramount to document workflow as an application's source code or API.

Along with grouping tools into categories based on the phases of building applications, it is also useful to group tools based on the opinions of a respective project—in our case, Angular, Ionic, and Firebase. I call tools grouped into opinionated workflows tool stacks. For example, the remainder of this chapter discusses the tool stack used to build the application that we will deploy across environments in this book. In contrast, if you were to build a Ruby on Rails application, the tool stack would be completely different because the project's opinions are different. Our app is called krakn, and it functions as a real-time chat application built on top of the opinions of Angular, the Ionic Framework, and Firebase.

You can find all of krakn's source code at `github.com/zachmoreno/krakn`.

Version control with Git and GitHub

Git is a **command-line interface (CLI)** developed by Linus Torvalds, to use on the famed Linux kernel. Git is mostly popular due to its distributed architecture making it nearly impossible for corruption to occur. Git's distributed architecture means that any remote repository has all of the same information as your local repository. It is useful to think of Git as a free insurance policy for my code.

```
C:\Users\zmoreno\Documents\GitHub\krakn (krakn)
λ git log --oneline
19e92d9 Added Gitter Chat badge
fcf27a7 receivedTime was not accurate if view is dormate then message submitted so I moved the new Date object
c64131e removed back button - thanks @AlexWhedbee
9c7f264 added message.receivedTime, added timeago filter, added time to view with associated styles, wip $ionic
41c8f73 split $scope.auth.user.email on @ & now syncing everything before the @ as username for a little bit mo
09ea30a Finally got Firebase to sync message.user as $rootScope.auth.user.email
f938518 wip {{ message.user }}
```

You will need to install Git using the instructions provided at `www.git-scm.com/book/en/Getting-Started-Installing-Git` for your development workstation's operating system.

`www.GitHub.com` has played a notable role in Git's popularization, turning its functionality into a social network focused on open source code contributions. With a pricing model that incentivizes Open Source contributions and licensing for private, GitHub elevated the use of Git to heights never seen before.

If you don't already have an account on GitHub, now is the perfect time to visit
`www.github.com` to provision a free account. I mentioned earlier that krakn's
code is available for forking at `www.github.com/zachmoreno/krakn`. This means
that any person with a GitHub account has the ability to view my version of krakn,
and clone a copy of their own for further modifications or contributions. In GitHub's
web application, forking manifests itself as a button located to the right of the
repository's title, which in this case is `ZachMoreno/krakn`. When you click on the
button, you will see an animation that simulates the hardcore forking action. This
results in a cloned repository under your account that will have a title to the tune
of `YourName/krakn`.

Node.js

Node.js, commonly known as Node, is a community-driven server environment built
on Google Chrome's V8 JavaScript runtime that is entirely event driven and facilitates
a nonblocking I/O model. According to `www.nodejs.org`, it is best suited for:

> *"Data-intensive real-time applications that run across distributed devices."*

So what does all this boil down to? Node empowers web developers to write
JavaScript both on the client and server with bidirectional real-time I/O. The advent
of Node has empowered developers to take their skills from the client to the server,
evolving from frontend to full stack (like a caterpillar evolving into a butterfly). Not
only do these skills facilitate a pay increase, they also advance the Web towards the
same functionality as the traditional desktop or native application.

For our purposes, we use Node as a tool; a tool to build real-time applications in
the fewest number of keystrokes, videos watched, and words read as possible. Node
is, in fact, a modular tool through its extensible package interface, called **Node
Package Manager** (**NPM**). You will use NPM as a means to install the remainder of
our tool stack.

NPM

The NPM is a means to install Node packages on your local or remote server. NPM is how we will install the majority of the tools and software used in this book. This is achieved by running the `$ npm install -g [PackageName]` command in your command line or terminal. To search the full list of Node packages, visit `www.npmjs.org` or run `$ npm search [Search Term]` in your command line or terminal as shown in the following screenshot:

```
C:\Users\zmoreno\Documents\GitHub\krakn (krakn)
npm search ionicjs
NAME            DESCRIPTION                    AUTHOR      DATE        VERSION KEYWORDS

generator-      A generator for the Ionic Framework =diegonetto 2014-04-15 0.2.5    yeoman-generator ionic fra
```

Yeoman's workflow

Yeoman is a CLI that is the glue that holds your tools into your opinionated workflow. Although the term opinionated might sound off-putting, you must first consider the wisdom and experience of the developers and community before you who maintain Yeoman. In this context, opinionated means a little more than a collection of the best practices that are all aimed at improving your developer's experience of building static websites, single page applications, and everything in between. Opinionated does not mean that you are locked into what someone else feels is best for you, nor does it mean that you must strictly adhere to the opinions or best practices included. Yeoman is general enough to help you build nearly anything for the Web as well as improving your workflow while developing it. The tools that make up Yeoman's workflow are Yo, Grunt.js, Bower, and a few others that are more-or-less optional, but are probably worth your time.

Yo

Apart from having one of the hippest namespaces, Yo is a powerful code generator that is intelligent enough to scaffold most sites and applications. By default, instantiating a yo command assumes that you mean to scaffold something at a project level, but yo can also be scoped more granularly by means of sub-generators. For example, the command for instantiating a new vanilla Angular project is as follows:

```
$ yo angular radicalApp
```

Yo will not finish your request until you provide some further information about your desired Angular project. This is achieved by asking you a series of relevant questions, and based on your answers, yo will scaffold a familiar application folder/file structure, along with all the boilerplate code. Note that if you have worked with the angular-seed project, then the Angular application that yo generates will look very familiar to you. Once you have an Angular app scaffolded, you can begin using sub-generator commands. The following command scaffolds a new route, `radicalRoute`, within `radicalApp`:

```
$ yo angular:route radicalRoute
```

The `:route` sub-generator is a very powerful command, as it automates all of the following key tasks:

- It creates a new file, `radicalApp/scripts/controllers/radicalRoute.js`, that contains the controller logic for the `radicalRoute` view

- It creates another new file, `radicalApp/views/radicalRoute.html`, that contains the associated view markup and directives

- Lastly, it adds an additional route within, `radicalApp/scripts/app.js`, that connects the view to the controller

Additionally, the sub-generators for `yo angular` include the following:

`:controller`

`:directive`

`:filter`

`:service`

`:provider`

`:factory`

`:value`

`:constant`

`:decorator`

`:view`

All the sub-generators allow you to execute finer detailed commands for scaffolding smaller components when compared to `:route`, which executes a combination of sub-generators.

Installing Yo

Within your workstation's terminal or command-line application type, insert the following command, followed by a return:

```
$ npm install -g yo
```

 If you are a Linux or Mac user, you might want to prefix the command with sudo, as follows:
```
$ sudo npm install -g yo
```

Grunt

Grunt.js is a task runner that enhances your existing and/or Yeoman's workflow by automating repetitive tasks. Each time you generate a new project with yo, it creates a /Gruntfile.js file that wires up all of the curated tasks. You might have noticed that installing Yo also installs all of Yo's dependencies. Reading through /Gruntfile.js should incite a fair amount of awe, as it gives you a snapshot of what is going on under the hood of Yeoman's curated Grunt tasks and its dependencies.

Generating a vanilla Angular app produces a /Gruntfile.js file, as it is responsible for performing the following tasks:

- It defines where Yo places Bower packages, which is covered in the next section

- It defines the path where the grunt build command places the production-ready code

- It initializes the watch task to run:
    - JSHint when JavaScript files are saved
    - Karma's test runner when JavaScript files are saved
    - Compass when SCSS or SASS files are saved
    - The saved /Gruntfile.js file

- It initializes LiveReload when any HTML or CSS files are saved

- It configures the grunt server command to run a Node.js server on localhost:9000, or to show test results on localhost:9001

- It autoprefixes CSS rules on LiveReload and grunt build

- It renames files for optimizing browser caching

- It configures the grunt build command to minify images, SVG, HTML, and CSS files or to safely minify Angular files

Let us pause for a moment to reflect on the amount of time it would take to find, learn, and implement each dependency into our existing workflow for each project we undertake. Ok, we should now have a greater appreciation for Yeoman and its community.

For the vast majority of the time, you will likely only use a few Grunt commands, which include the following:

```
$ grunt server
$ grunt test
$ grunt build
```

Bower

If Yo scaffolds our application's structure and files, and Grunt automates repetitive tasks for us, then what does Bower bring to the party? Bower is web development's missing package manager. Its functionality parallels that of Ruby Gems for the Ruby on Rails MVC framework, but is not limited to any single framework or technology stack. The explicit use of Bower is not required by the Yeoman workflow, but as I mentioned previously, the use of Bower is configured automatically for you in your project's /Gruntfile.js file.

How does managing packages improve our development workflow? With all of the time we've been spending in our command lines and terminals, it is handy to have the ability to automate the management of third-party dependencies within our application. This ability manifests itself in a few simple commands, the most ubiquitous being the following command:

```
$ bower install [PackageName] --save
```

With this command, Bower will automate the following steps:

1. First, search its packages for the specified package name
2. Download the latest stable version of the package if found
3. Move the package to the location defined in your project's /Gruntfile.js file, typically a folder named /bower_components
4. Insert dependencies in the form of <link> elements for CSS files in the document's <head> element, and <script> elements for JavaScript files right above the document's closing </body> tag, to the package's files within your project's /index.html file

This process is one that web developers are more than familiar with because adding a JavaScript library or new dependency happens multiple times within every project. Bower speeds up our existing manual process through automation and improves it by providing the latest stable version of a package and then notifying us of an update if one is available. This last part, "notifying us of an update if … available", is important because as a web developer advances from one project to the next, it is easy to overlook keeping dependencies as up to date as possible. This is achieved by running the following command:

```
$ bower update
```

This command returns all the available updates, if available, and will go through the same process of inserting new references where applicable.

Bower.io includes all of the documentation on how to use Bower to its fullest potential along with the ability to search through all of the available Bower packages.

> Searching for available Bower packages can also be achieved by running the following command:
>
> ```
> $ bower search [SearchTerm]
> ```
>
> If you cannot find the specific dependency for which you search, and the project is on GitHub, consider contributing a bower.json file to the project's root and inviting the owner to register it by running the following command:
>
> ```
> $ bower register [ThePackageName] [GitEndpoint]
> ```
>
> Registration allows you to install your dependency by running the next command:
>
> ```
> $ bower install [ThePackageName]
> ```

The Ionic framework

The Ionic framework is a truly remarkable advancement in bridging the gap between web applications and native mobile applications. In some ways, Ionic parallels Yeoman where it assembles tools that were already available to developers into a neat package, and structures a workflow around them, inherently improving our experience as developers.

If Ionic is analogous to Yeoman, then what are the tools that make up Ionic's workflow? The tools that, when combined, make Ionic noteworthy are Apache Cordova, Angular, Ionic's suite of Angular directives, and Ionic's mobile UI framework.

Batarang

An invaluable piece to our Angular tool stack is the Google Chrome Developer Tools extension, Batarang, by Brian Ford. Batarang adds a third-party panel (on the right-hand side of **Console**) to DevTools that facilitates Angular's specific inspection in the event of debugging. We can view data in the scopes of each model, analyze each expression's performance, and view a beautiful visualization of service dependencies all from within Batarang. Because Angular augments the DOM with ng- attributes, it also provides a **Properties** pane within the **Elements** panel, to inspect the models attached to a given element's scope. The extension is easy to install from either the Chrome Web Store or the project's GitHub repository and inspection can be enabled by performing the following steps:

1. Firstly, open the Chrome Developer Tools.
2. You should then navigate to the AngularJS panel.
3. Finally, select the **Enable** checkbox on the far right tab.

Your active Chrome tab will then be reloaded automatically, and the **AngularJS** panel will begin populating the inspection data. In addition, you can leverage the **Angular** pane with the **Elements** panel to view Angular-specific properties at an elemental level, and observe the $scope variable from within the **Console** panel.

Sublime Text and Editor integration

While developing any Angular app, it is helpful to augment our workflow further with Angular-specific syntax completion, snippets, go to definition, and quick panel search in the form of a Sublime Text package. Perform the following steps:

1. If you haven't installed Sublime Text already, you need to first install Package Control. Otherwise, continue with the next step.
2. Once installed, press *command* + *Shift* + *P* in Sublime.
3. Then, you need to select the **Package Control: Install Package** option.
4. Finally, type angularjs and press *Enter* on your keyboard.

In addition to support within Sublime, Angular enhancements exist for lots of popular editors, including WebStorm, Coda, and TextMate.

Krakn

As a quick refresher, krakn was constructed using all of the tools that are covered in this chapter. These include Git, GitHub, Node.js, NPM, Yeoman's workflow, Yo, Grunt, Bower, Batarang, and Sublime Text. The application builds on Angular, Firebase, the Ionic Framework, and a few other minor dependencies.

The workflow I used to develop krakn went something like the following. Follow these steps to achieve the same thing. Note that you can skip the remainder of this section if you'd like to get straight to the deployment action, and feel free to rename things where necessary.

Setting up Git and GitHub

The workflow I followed while developing krakn begins with initializing our local Git repository and connecting it to our remote master repository on GitHub. In order to install and set up both, perform the following steps:

1. Firstly, install all the tool stack dependencies, and create a folder called `krakn`.

2. Following this, run `$ git init`, and you will create a `README.md` file.

3. You should then run `$ git add README.md` and commit `README.md` to the local master branch.

4. You then need to create a new remote repository on GitHub called `ZachMoreno/krakn`.

5. Following this, run the following command:

    ```
    $ git remote add origin git@github.com:[YourGitHubUserName] /
    krakn.git
    ```

6. Conclude the setup by running `$ git push -u origin master`.

Scaffolding the app with Yo

Scaffolding our app couldn't be easier with the `yo ionic` generator. To do this, perform the following steps:

1. Firstly, install Yo by running `$ npm install -g yo`.

2. After this, install `generator-ionicjs` by running `$ npm install -g generator-ionicjs`.

3. To conclude the scaffolding of your application, run the `yo ionic` command.

Development

After scaffolding the folder structure and boilerplate code, our workflow advances to the development phase, which is encompassed in the following steps:

1. To begin, run `grunt server`.
2. You are now in a position to make changes, for example, these being deletions or additions.
3. Once these are saved, LiveReload will automatically reload your browser.
4. You can then review the changes in the browser.
5. Repeat steps 2-4 until you are ready to advance to the predeployment phase.

Views, controllers, and routes

Being a simple chat application, krakn has only a handful of views/routes. They are login, chat, account, menu, and about. The menu view is present in all the other views in the form of an off-canvas menu.

The login view

The default view/route/controller is named login. The login view utilizes the Firebase's Simple Login feature to authenticate users before proceeding to the rest of the application. Apart from logging into krakn, users can register a new account by entering their desired credentials. An interesting part of the login view is the use of the `ng-show` directive to toggle the second password field if the user selects the register button. However, the `ng-model` directive is the first step here, as it is used to pass the input text from the view to the controller and ultimately, the Firebase Simple Login. Other than the Angular magic, this view uses the `ion-view` directive, grid, and buttons that are all core to Ionic.

Each view within an Ionic app is wrapped within an `ion-view` directive that contains a `title` attribute as follows:

```
<ion-view title="Login">
```

The login view uses the standard input elements that contain a `ng-model` attribute to bind the input's value back to the controller's `$scope` as follows:

```
<input type="text" placeholder="you@email.com" ng-model=
"data.email" />

<input type="password" placeholder=
"embody strength" ng-model="data.pass" />
```

```
<input type="password" placeholder=
"embody strength" ng-model="data.confirm" />
```

The `Log In` and `Register` buttons call their respective functions using the `ng-click` attribute, with the value set to the function's name as follows:

```
<button class="button button-block button-positive" ng-
click="login()" ng-hide="createMode">Log In</button>
```

The `Register` and `Cancel` buttons set the value of `$scope.createMode` to `true` or `false` to show or hide the correct buttons for either action:

```
<button class="button button-block button-calm" ng-
click="createMode = true" ng-hide=
"createMode">Register</button>
<button class="button button-block button-calm" ng-
show="createMode" ng-click=
"createAccount()">Create Account</button>

<button class="button button-block button-
assertive" ng-show="createMode" ng-click="createMode =
false">Cancel</button>
```

`$scope.err` is displayed only when you want to show the feedback to the user:

```
<p ng-show="err" class="assertive text-center">{{err}}</p>

</ion-view>
```

The login controller is dependent on Firebase's `loginService` module and Angular's core `$location` module:

```
controller('LoginCtrl', ['$scope', 'loginService', '$location',
    function($scope, loginService, $location) {
```

Ionic's directives tend to create isolated scopes, so it was useful here to wrap our controller's variables within a `$scope.data` object to avoid issues within the isolated scope as follows:

```
$scope.data = {
  "email"    : null,
  "pass"     : null,
  "confirm"  : null,
  "createMode" : false
}
```

The `login()` function easily checks the credentials before authentication and sends feedback to the user if needed:

```
$scope.login = function(cb) {
  $scope.err = null;
  if( !$scope.data.email ) {
    $scope.err = 'Please enter an email address';
  }
  else if( !$scope.data.pass ) {
    $scope.err = 'Please enter a password';
  }
```

If the credentials are sound, we send them to Firebase for authentication, and when we receive a success callback, we route the user to the chat view using `$location.path()` as follows:

```
  else {
    loginService.login($scope.data.email,
    $scope.data.pass, function(err, user) {
      $scope.err = err? err + '' : null;
      if( !err ) {
        cb && cb(user);
        $location.path('krakn/chat');
      }
    });
  }
};
```

The `createAccount()` function works in much the same way as `login()`, except that it ensures that the users don't already exist before adding them to your Firebase and logging them in:

```
$scope.createAccount = function() {
  $scope.err = null;
  if( assertValidLoginAttempt() ) {
    loginService.createAccount($scope.data.email,
$scope.data.pass,
      function(err, user) {
        if( err ) {
          $scope.err = err? err + '' : null;
        }
        else {
          // must be logged in before I can write to
my profile
          $scope.login(function() {
```

```
                  loginService.createProfile(user.uid,
      user.email);
                  $location.path('krakn/account');
              });
          }
        });
    }
  };
```

The `assertValidLoginAttempt()` function is a function used to ensure that no errors are received through the account creation and authentication flows:

```
function assertValidLoginAttempt() {
  if( !$scope.data.email ) {
    $scope.err = 'Please enter an email address';
  }
  else if( !$scope.data.pass ) {
    $scope.err = 'Please enter a password';
  }
  else if( $scope.data.pass !== $scope.data.confirm ) {
    $scope.err = 'Passwords do not match';
  }
  return !$scope.err;
}
}])
```

The chat view

Keeping vegan practices aside, the meat and potatoes of krakn's functionality lives within the chat view/controller/route. The design is similar to most SMS clients, with the input in the footer of the view and messages listed chronologically in the main content area. The `ng-repeat` directive is used to display a message every time a message is added to the messages collection in Firebase. If you submit a message successfully, unsuccessfully, or without any text, feedback is provided via the placeholder attribute of the message input.

There are two filters being utilized within the chat view: `orderByPriority` and `timeAgo`. The `orderByPriority` filter is defined within the `firebase` module that uses the Firebase object IDs that ensure objects are always chronological.

 The `timeAgo` filter is an open source Angular module that I found. You can access it at www.jsfiddle.net/i_woody/cnL5T/.

The `ion-view` directive is used once again to contain our chat view:

```
<ion-view title="Chat">
```

Our list of messages is composed using the `ion-list` and `ion-item` directives, in addition to a couple of key attributes. The `ion-list` directive gives us some nice interactive controls using the `option-buttons` and `can-swipe` attributes. This results in each list item being swipable to the left, revealing our `option-buttons` as follows:

```
<ion-list option-buttons="itemButtons" can-swipe=
    "true" ng-show="messages">
```

Our workhorse in the chat view is the trusty `ng-repeat` directive, responsible for persisting our data from Firebase to our service to our controller and into our view and back again:

```
<ion-item ng-repeat="message in messages |
    orderByPriority" item="item" can-swipe="true">
```

Then, we bind our data into vanilla HTML elements that have some custom styles applied to them:

```
<h2 class="user">{{ message.user }}</h2>
```

The third-party `timeago` filter converts the time into something such as, "5 min ago", similar to Instagram or Facebook:

```
<small class="time">{{ message.receivedTime |
    timeago }}</small>
<p class="message">{{ message.text }}</p>
</ion-item>
</ion-list>
```

A vanilla input element is used to accept chat messages from our users. The input data is bound to `$scope.data.newMessage` for sending data to Firebase and `$scope.feedback` is used to keep our users informed:

```
<input type="text" class="{{ feeling }}" placeholder=
    "{{ feedback }}" ng-model="data.newMessage" />
```

When you click on the `send`/`submit` button, the `addMessage()` function sends the message to your Firebase, and adds it to the list of chat messages, in real time:

```
<button type="submit" id="chat-send" class="button button-small
button-clear" ng-click="addMessage()"><span class="ion-android-
send"></span></button>
</ion-view>
```

The `ChatCtrl` controller is dependant on a few more modules other than our `LoginCtrl`, including `syncData`, `$ionicScrollDelegate`, `$ionicLoading`, and `$rootScope`:

```
controller('ChatCtrl', ['$scope', 'syncData', '$ionicScrollDelegate',
'$ionicLoading', '$rootScope',
    function($scope, syncData, $ionicScrollDelegate, $ionicLoading,
$rootScope) {
```

The `userName` variable is derived from the authenticated user's e-mail address (saved within the application's `$rootScope`) by splitting the e-mail and using everything before the `@` symbol:

```
var userEmail = $rootScope.auth.user.e-mail
    userName = userEmail.split('@');
```

Avoid isolated scope issue in the same fashion, as we did in `LoginCtrl`:

```
$scope.data = {
  newMessage   : null,
  user         : userName[0]
}
```

Our view will only contain the latest 20 messages that have been synced from Firebase:

```
$scope.messages = syncData('messages', 20);
```

When a new message is saved/synced, it is added to the bottom of the `ng-repeated` list, so we use the `$ionicScrollDeligate` variable to automatically scroll the new message into view on the display as follows:

```
$ionicScrollDelegate.scrollBottom(true);
```

Our default chat input placeholder text is `something on your mind?`:

```
$scope.feedback = 'something on your mind?';
// displays as class on chat input placeholder
$scope.feeling = 'stable';
```

If we have a new message and a valid username (shortened), then we can call the `$add()` function, which syncs the new message to Firebase and our view is as follows:

```
$scope.addMessage = function() {
  if( $scope.data.newMessage
    && $scope.data.user ) {
    // new data elements cannot be synced without adding
      them to FB Security Rules
    $scope.messages.$add({
            text    : $scope.data.newMessage,
```

```
                user      : $scope.data.user,
                receivedTime : Number(new Date())
            });
    // clean up
    $scope.data.newMessage = null;
```

On a successful sync, the feedback updates say Done! What's next?, as shown in the following code snippet:

```
    $scope.feedback = 'Done! What\'s next?';
    $scope.feeling = 'stable';
  }
  else {
    $scope.feedback = 'Please write a message before sending';
    $scope.feeling = 'assertive';
  }
};

    $ionicScrollDelegate.scrollBottom(true);
])
```

The account view

The account view allows the logged in users to view their current name and e-mail address along with providing them with the ability to update their password and e-mail address. The input fields interact with Firebase in the same way as the chat view does using the syncData method defined in the firebase module:

```
<ion-view title="'Account'" left-buttons="leftButtons">
```

The $scope.user object contains our logged in user's account credentials, and we bind them into our view as follows:

```
<p>{{ user.name }}</p>
...
<p>{{ user.email }}</p>
```

The basic account management functionality is provided within this view; so users can update their e-mail address and or password if they choose to, using the following code snippet:

```
<input type="password" ng-keypress=
  "reset()" ng-model="oldpass"/>
...
<input type="password" ng-keypress=
  "reset()" ng-model="newpass"/>
...
```

```
<input type="password" ng-keypress=
  "reset()" ng-model="confirm"/>
```

Both the `updatePassword()` and `updateEmail()` functions work in much the same fashion as our `createAccount()` function within the `LoginCtrl` controller. They check whether the new e-mail or password is not the same as the old, and if all is well, it syncs them to Firebase and back again:

```
<button class="button button-block button-calm" ng-click=
  "updatePassword()">update password</button>
...

  <p class="error" ng-show="err">{{err}}</p>
<p class="good" ng-show="msg">{{msg}}</p>
...

  <input type="text" ng-keypress="reset()" ng-model="newemail"/>
...

  <input type="password" ng-keypress="reset()" ng-model="pass"/>
...

  <button class="button button-block button-calm" ng-click=
  "updateEmail()">update email</button>
...

  <p class="error" ng-show="emailerr">{{emailerr}}</p>
<p class="good" ng-show="emailmsg">{{emailmsg}}</p>
...
</ion-view>
```

The menu view

Within `krakn/app/scripts/app.js`, the menu route is defined as the only abstract state. Because of its abstract state, it can be presented in the app along with the other views by the `ion-side-menus` directive provided by Ionic. You might have noticed that only two menu options are available before signing into the application and that the rest appear only after authenticating. This is achieved using the `ng-show-auth` directive on the chat, account, and log out menu items. The majority of the options for Ionic's directives are available through attributes making them simple to use. For example, take a look at the `animation="slide-left-right"` attribute. You will find Ionic's use of custom attributes within the directives as one of the ways that the Ionic Framework is setting itself apart from other options within this space.

The `ion-side-menu` directive contains our menu list similarly to the one we previously covered, the `ion-view` directive, as follows:

```
<ion-side-menus>
  <ion-pane ion-side-menu-content>
    <ion-nav-bar class="bar-positive">
```

Our back button is displayed by including the `ion-nav-back-button` directive within the `ion-nav-bar` directive:

```
<ion-nav-back-button class="button-clear"><i class=
   "icon ion-chevron-left"></i> Back</ion-nav-back-button>
</ion-nav-bar>
```

Animations within Ionic are exposed and used through the `animation` attribute, which is built atop the `ngAnimate` module. In this case, we are doing a simple animation that replicates the experience of a native mobile app:

```
<ion-nav-view name="menuContent" animation="slide-left-right"></ion-
nav-view>
 </ion-pane>

 <ion-side-menu side="left">
  <header class="bar bar-header bar-positive">
   <h1 class="title">Menu</h1>
  </header>
  <ion-content class="has-header">
```

A simple `ion-list` directive/element is used to display our navigation items in a vertical list. The `ng-show` attribute handles the display of menu items before and after a user has authenticated. Before a user logs in, they can access the navigation, but only the About and Log In views are available until after successful authentication.

```
<ion-list>
 <ion-item nav-clear menu-close href=
   "#/app/chat" ng-show-auth="'login'">
  Chat
 </ion-item>

 <ion-item nav-clear menu-close href="#/app/about">
  About
 </ion-item>

 <ion-item nav-clear menu-close href=
   "#/app/login" ng-show-auth="['logout','error']">
  Log In
 </ion-item>
```

The Log Out navigation item is only displayed once logged in, and upon a click, it calls the `logout()` function in addition to navigating to the login view:

```
<ion-item nav-clear menu-close href="#/app/login" ng-click=
   "logout()" ng-show-auth="'login'">
  Log Out
```

```
        </ion-item>
      </ion-list>
    </ion-content>
  </ion-side-menu>
</ion-side-menus>
```

The `MenuCtrl` controller is the simplest controller in this application, as all it contains is the `toggleMenu()` and `logout()` functions:

```
controller("MenuCtrl", ['$scope', 'loginService', '$location',
  '$ionicScrollDelegate', function($scope, loginService,
  $location, $ionicScrollDelegate) {
  $scope.toggleMenu = function() {
    $scope.sideMenuController.toggleLeft();
  };

  $scope.logout = function() {
    loginService.logout();
    $scope.toggleMenu();   };
}])
```

The about view

The about view is 100 percent static, and its only real purpose is to present the credits for all the open source projects used in the application.

Global controller constants

All of krakn's controllers share only two dependencies: `ionic` and `ngAnimate`. Because Firebase's modules are defined within `/app/scripts/app.js`, they are available for consumption by all the controllers without the need to define them as dependencies. Therefore, the `firebase` service's `syncData` and `loginService` are available to `ChatCtrl` and `LoginCtrl` for use.

The `syncData` service is how krakn utilizes three-way data binding provided by `www.krakn.firebaseio.com`. For example, within the `ChatCtrl` controller, we use `syncData( 'messages', 20 )` to bind the latest twenty messages within the `messages` collection to `$scope` for consumption by the chat view. Conversely, when a `ng-click` user clicks the submit button, we write the data to the `messages` collection by use of the `syncData.$add()` method inside the `$scope.addMessage()` function:

```
$scope.addMessage = function() {
  if(...) { $scope.messages.$add({ ... });
  }
};
```

Models and services

The model for krakn is `www.krakn.firebaseio.com`. The services that consume krakn's Firebase API are as follows:

- The `firebase` service in `krakn/app/scripts/service.firebase.js`
- The `login` service in `krakn/app/scripts/service.login.js`
- The `changeEmail` service in `krakn/app/scripts/changeEmail.firebase.js`

The `firebase` service defines the `syncData` service that is responsible for routing data bidirectionally between `krakn/app/bower_components/angularfire.js` and our controllers. Please note that the reason I have not mentioned `angularfire.js` until this point is that it is basically an abstract data translation layer between `firebaseio.com` and Angular applications that intend on consuming data as a service.

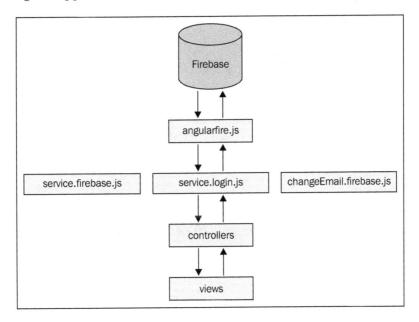

Predeployment

Once the majority of an application's development phase has been completed, at least for the initial launch, it is important to run all of the code through a build process that optimizes the file size through compression of images and minification of text files. This piece of the workflow was not overlooked by Yeoman and is available through the use of the `$ grunt build` command. As mentioned in the section on Grunt, the `/Gruntfile.js` file defines where built code is placed once it is optimized for deployment. Yeoman's default location for built code is the `/dist` folder, which might or might not exist depending on whether you have run the `grunt build` command before.

Summary

In this chapter, we discussed the tool stack and workflow used to build the app that we will deploy in the forthcoming chapters. Together, Git and Yeoman formed a solid foundation for building krakn. Git and GitHub provided us with distributed version control and a platform for sharing the application's source code with you and the world. Yeoman facilitated the remainder of the workflow: scaffolding with Yo, automation with Grunt, and package management with Bower. With our app fully scaffolded, we were able to build our interface with the directives provided by the Ionic Framework, and wire up the real-time data synchronization forged by our Firebase instance. With a few key tools, we were able to minimize our development time while maximizing our return.

Next, we will take our freshly constructed real-time chat app, krakn, and deploy it to an Apache web server for consumption over the Web. Once manually deployed to Apache, we will discuss automating future deployments and optimizing the environment for an Angular application.

2
Deploying to Apache

The Apache HTTP server is without a doubt the most common destination for websites and applications being deployed into production. Because of this, most developers have some level of comfort with deploying to a remote Apache server, but will likely have limited experience in deploying an Angular application to this server environment. Take a look at the graph in the following figure to see how Apache stacks up when compared to other top servers:

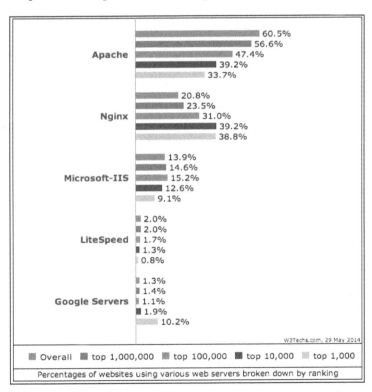

Source: http://w3techs.com/technologies/cross/web_server/ranking

In this chapter, we will cover the following points:

- Things needed to properly host an Angular app on an Apache server
- To deploy to a remote Apache server using both the FTP CLI and clients
- To automate deployment with GitHub Service Hooks and SSH
- To optimize Apache's configuration to support the use of Google's PageSpeed Service and Angular's HTML5Mode
- To avoid some gotchas and pitfalls along the way

From local to remote

Prior to automating segments of your workflow, it is valuable to traverse the flow manually to ensure that all phases are accounted for, and to minimize variables in the process. Most developers have likely deployed source code to either local or remote Apache servers alike, and because of that I will attempt to focus my efforts on the gotchas and nuances that apply to applications written in Angular.

Up until this point, we have conducted all local development on a Node.js server, provided by running the `grunt server` command from within our application's root directory. To clarify any possible confusion caused by this divergence, Angular is designed to be server agnostic, and therefore can be served from almost any backend stack you like, including Apache. Because of Angular's server agnostic design, it is fully possible to develop Angular applications locally served from Apache. I encourage a local Node.js server over Apache, because the developer experience of JavaScript on the client and server is improved by not introducing alternate syntax and possible confusion therein.

Deployment destination

All web servers share a constant pattern, which is a single root directory where all sites or applications are served from. Apache's root directory is typically named `/public_html`. This will be the remote location where we upload all application source code and resource.

Apache can look at a different directory as its root if you so configure. To do so, open /etc/apache2/conf/httpd. conf in your text editor of choice (Sublime Text will do nicely). Then look for two lines that are the same or very similar to:

```
DocumentRoot "/etc/lampp/public_html"
<Directory "/etc/lampp/public_html">
```

Here, you can change the path and/or root folder name to whatever you desire. Remember that your changes will not take effect until you restart Apache.

A comparison between the local and remote setup

Be mindful of the differences between your local and remote Apache environmental configurations. For example, local development environment tools such as XAMPP, MAMPP, and WAMPP often change the default document root directory's name from /public_html (remote) to /htdocs (local). You will most likely find that this matters very little in your workflow overall, but it can cause notable confusion. Beyond the aforementioned difference, it is useful to run both your local and remote httpd.conf files through a different tool (see the *Troubleshooting deployment issues* section for more details) to ensure they are configured as you intend.

Manual deployment

Now that we know Apache will watch our remote /public_html directory, we can move forward by uploading our files to that location. The most common way of publishing your files to a remote web server is by use of the **File Transfer Protocol (FTP)**. FTP can be achieved through a CLI that lives within the core of all operating systems, both open source and licensed. It is common, however, to utilize an FTP client, to again, improve your developer experience. Applications such as the free FileZilla and licensed Transmit provide a highly usable interface for dragging and dropping files from your development workstation onto your remote server, a pattern that most people are comfortable with.

FTPing from your command line

At some point, you may feel that using the command line is a grueling process in comparison to an interface, but it has its benefits, speed mainly, and the `ftp` command is no exception. We begin by running the `ftp` command followed by the IP address of our destination server as follows:

```
ftp 123.4.5.678
```

Take notice that your prompt has changed to reflect that you are indeed conducting an FTP session. It should read `ftp>` below the previous command. Initiating an FTP session will typically connect you at your server's root directory, which is not where we intend to deploy our application. Therefore, we must change directories by utilizing the following command:

```
ftp> cd path/to/your/public_html
```

The CLI will then provide you with feedback of either a success or failure, along with your new location.

> If your session is ever interrupted and you need to leave your machine in order to come back later, it is handy to know the current location of your FTP session. To do so, employ the following command:
>
> ```
> ftp> pwd
> ```

Once connected via FTP to your remote server and within the `/public_html` directory, you can deploy `krakn` to your remote Apache server. Before doing so, we must first ensure that we are within our local version of `krakn`. While connected to FTP, you can change your workstation location by using the `ftp> lcd` command, as follows:

```
ftp> lcd /location/of/your/local/krakn/dist
```

> My tendency is to place all cloned Git repositories within a single folder on my desktop, resulting in a structure similar to `~/Desktop/clones/krakn/dist`. Remember that `/dist` is the location where Grunt places post-build files and resources that are optimized for deployment.

Our FTP deployment workflow will be as follows:

1. Firstly, you need to create a new directory named krakn.

2. You can then change the remote working directory to /krakn.

3. To conclude, put all files from /location/of/your/local/krakn/dist to /your/remote/apache/server/public_html.

The previous workflow has all been made possible by running the following commands:

```
ftp> mkdir krakn
ftp> cd krakn
ftp> mput *
```

The FTP mput command behaves the same as the standard put command except that you can publish multiple files in one command, while * is interpreted as all files (or sometimes referred to as a "wildcard"). The CLI will again provide feedback on success or failure, so you do not have to go through and manually inspect that all files are indeed present and accounted for on your remote server. Once your files have been deployed successfully, you can exit the FTP CLI by running the following command:

```
ftp> close
```

FTP clients

The two FTP clients I mentioned earlier are just two of the larger fish in a fairly large pond. FileZilla is very popular because of its lack of cost, while Transmit (OS X only) comes at a fair price and delivers a highly polished UI. All FTP clients improve upon the CLI by improving the development experience of the following:

- Navigating to your own local folders and resources
- Connecting to your remote server
- Navigating to your remote destination folder, /public_html
- Drag-and-drop for upload and download

The following is a screenshot of Panic's Transmit FTP client. From looking at this, you can see how Transmit provides a sleek interface for FTPing your files to your remote server environment. The interface in most FTP clients divides the layout into two columns. The left column is most often the local hard drive file system navigator, while the right is the remote server file system navigator. Once your two destinations have been selected, you can select your files on the left and drag them to the right for uploading as shown in the following screenshot:

(source: `http://panic.com/transmit/`)

They all tend to further augment the upload process by providing you with the ability to intelligently upload or download files. Take for example, that you are deploying Version 2.0 of krakn, or any other application, and you do not want to worry about which files were changed and which files were not, before uploading. FileZilla will allow you to select everything and drop them on the remote server. FTP clients will typically ask you what action you'd like to take on overwriting duplicate files or not. You have the option to overwrite existing files, overwrite if the source files are newer, overwrite if different size, rename the new files, or skip over them all together.

This is extremely handy as it provides a level of granularity to your upload or download that is not possible with the core FTP CLI. Other useful features provided by many FTP clients are the ability to see what, if any, files failed to upload in real-time, with the reason for the failure, and the ability to save connection settings for reuse. The latter feature is really simple but it is a feature that the CLI lacks. Furthermore, the saved connections are typically exportable and importable, as is the case in FileZilla.

Automating deployment with GitHub and SSH

GitHub's features go well beyond distributed version control in the cloud, which is amazing in itself. In the settings for each repository hosted on GitHub, there is a section entitled "Service Hooks". This provides an interface to automate a reaction every time a specified action takes place. For instance, you can effectively tell GitHub whenever I push to my remote master repository (the action) to do "something" (the reaction). In our case, that "something" will be to run a specific .PHP file on your remote Apache server that initiates a git pull from the same repository. The developer and blogger, Jeffrey Way, first documented this technique in an article and video he published (which you can access at http://goo.gl/qgFyg4) on the tutorial site tutsplus.com (which was formerly nettuts.com). We will explore configuring your remote Git repository for deployment whenever you complete a push to the remote master repository.

 Note that you will need to attain SSH access to your remote Apache server to complete this automation. Attaining SSH access to your server will vary from hosting provider to provider, so it is best to simply Google "yourWebHost+SSH" to find hosting-specific instructions.

1. Once SSHed into your server, you will need to generate a new SSH public key for your remote server environment, to securely communicate with your GitHub repository. This is achieved by running the following command on your server:

    ```
    $ ssh-keygen -t rsa -C "your_email@example.com"
    ```

2. Then you will be asked to create and verify a new passphrase for the newly created SSH public key as follows:

    ```
    Enter passphrase (empty for no passphrase): [Type a passphrase]
    Enter same passphrase again: [Type passphrase again]
    ```

3. When the passphrase has been successfully assigned, you will receive the following response:

   ```
   Your identification has been saved in /Users/you/.ssh/id_rsa.

   Your public key has been saved in /Users/you/.ssh/id_rsa.pub.

   The key fingerprint is: # 01:0f:f4:3b:ca:85:d6:17:a1:7d:f0:68:9d:f
   0:a2:db your_email@example.com
   ```

4. To fully add the new SSH public key to your Apache server's SSH-agent, run the following command:

   ```
   ssh-add ~/.ssh/id_rsa
   ```

5. We will then copy the newly created SSH key to our local clipboard for use on `GitHub.com` as follows:

   ```
   pbcopy < ~/.ssh/id_rsa.pub
   ```

To complete the secure connection between your remote apache server and GitHub, you will need to add the newly created/copied SSH public key to your GitHub account. To do so perform the following steps:

1. Firstly, select the global **Account Settings** link that is always present near the right side of GitHub's navigation.
2. You then need to select the **SSH Keys** menu item within the left sidebar of the **Account Settings** page.
3. Now select the **Add SSH Key** button, enter a descriptive name for your remote Apache server, and paste in your newly created SSH public key.
4. Finally, clicking on the **Add Key** button will prompt a verification of your GitHub password. Now GitHub and your remote Apache server can send data to-and-fro, using the SSH protocol.

Following this, we will enable GitHub service hooks from within our repository's settings. To do so perform the following steps:

1. You should first navigate to the root of your repository on `GitHub.com`, something similar to `https://github.com/YourName/krakn`.
2. On the left of the page select the **Settings** menu item, just above the **SSH clone URL**. Then, select the third menu item within the **Settings** view that reads **Webhooks and Services**. GitHub defines these services as "pre-built integrations that perform certain actions when events occur on GitHub."

3. Next, select the **Add Service** button so that we can select the **Post-Receive URLs** option from the drop-down menu. At this point in time you have no URL to paste into the **Post-Receive URL** field, so you will need to create a new file within the root of your repository called `github-pull.php`. The contents of which is only a single line of PHP code as follows:

```
<?php `git pull`; ?>
```

The above code will execute the `git pull` shell command for you from your remote Apache server, which is exactly the desired reaction you want to execute whenever you push to your GitHub repository.

4. You will then need to upload the `github-pull.php` file to your server with either FTP or by SSHing into your server and running a Git clone and pull of your desired repository. Once present on your remote Apache server in the location you'd like to automatically pull your repository, you will need to figure out the exact URL of the `github-pull.php` file that is now on your server.

5. Once you have the URL copied to your local clipboard, you can return to your GitHub Post-Receive settings to paste in the URL of your `github-pull.php` file. Now each time you push updates to your remote repository, GitHub will run your PHP code on your remote Apache server and automatically pull in the latest code.

Troubleshooting deployment issues

It is nearly inevitable that there will someday be an issue within your deployment workflow. These issues can range from something as simple as forgetting to include a file in your `put`, or as complex as overriding your environmental configuration. Whatever the issue may be, it is best to have a contingency plan for this rainy day. Tools are ever your friends, troubleshooting included. The cornerstone of any deployment issue is a bulletproof diff tool. Diff tools allow you to compare the contents of two files or folders. Take, for example, you mistakenly published an old version of your application. You could use a diff tool to compare your local development source code with your remote production source code to tell you which files are out of place. Most diff tools sport similar interfaces that allow you to select two folders or two files to compare against each other. Diff tools are like using a magnet to find a needle in a haystack; they will narrow the issue to a manageable focus.

A visual diff tool

Meld is an open source diff and merge tool that runs cross platform, and supports both folders and files alike. To download Meld for your development environment navigate to `http://meldmerge.org/`.

You can see in the following screenshot, the file directory for Meld. Most tools like Meld offer a similar interface to the one you saw previously. The interface is typically divided in half, with the left containing the file or folder that is the original, and the right containing the file or folder you are comparing it to. Deleted lines or files are displayed on the right in red for deleted, and green for added as shown in the following screenshot:

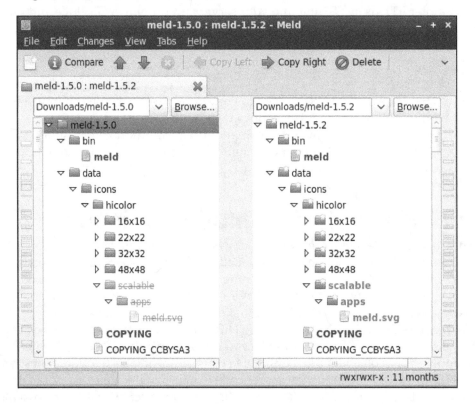

Using diff with Git

If you find yourself in the trenches of a deployment catastrophe without tools, and you are using Git, you can run a diff on two commits from the command line. To diff with Git, run the following command in your terminal or command line:

```
$ git diff <commit> <commit>
```

or

```
$ git diff <commit> -- <path>
```

The output will resemble the following screenshot. Similar to most visual diff tools, Git diff provides you with a line-for-line/file-for-file breakdown of what has been added or deleted. Additions are displayed as green with a prepended +, while deletions are displayed as red with a prepended - as shown in the following screenshot:

```
krakn — less — 80×24
diff --git a/app/scripts/app.js b/app/scripts/app.js
index 38d28af..953156b 100644
--- a/app/scripts/app.js
+++ b/app/scripts/app.js
@@ -24,11 +24,11 @@ angular.module('Krakn', [
               $location,
               $ionicScrollDelegate) {

-    $ionicPlatform.ready(function() {
-      if(window.StatusBar) {
-        StatusBar.styleDefault();
-      }
-    });
+    // $ionicPlatform.ready(function() {
+    //    if(window.StatusBar) {
+    //      StatusBar.styleDefault();
+    //    }
+    // });

    if( FBURL === 'https://INSTANCE.firebaseio.com' ) {
      // double-check that the app has been configured
```

Configuring Apache for Angular

Angular applications can run well when served by Apache under its default configuration, but there is undoubtedly room for improvements, both Angular specific and otherwise. We will explore adding a third-party module to extend Apache's default global functionality, while adding some rewrite rules to support the use of the HTML5 History API within your Angular application.

> Note that Apache can be configured in many varying ways to support all types of infrastructures and applications. Before modifying any of Apache's configurations within a production environment, please consult with your network or server administrators. If you are a full-stack developer, then you should be good to go!

Google's PageSpeed Service for Apache

Optimizing a website or application is a science unto its own and people spend the majority of their careers striving to shave off milliseconds or clean up jank (animation stutters). There are well-documented best practices that all web developers should follow less than 60 frames per second to some degree, but tools exist to achieve big gains with minimal effort. Google's PageSpeed Service is one of these tools. It works by attempting to automate a lot of best practices on the server, before the files are delivered to the client. For example, an image file in production has not been optimized or compressed. PageSpeed Service will optimize or compress it for you, before it is delivered to your users.

Google PageSpeed, according to `https://developers.google.com/speed/pagespeed/`, is described as a

> *"family of tools [that] is designed to help you optimize the performance of your website."*

It is useful to think of Google PageSpeed as a postdeployment tool stack for optimizing the delivery of your code, similar to Grunt's build process, but executed on the server side. The Apache HTTP Server is extensible through modules, and PageSpeed can be utilized as an Apache module. `mod_pagespeed` is one tool in the suite that, according to `https://developers.google.com/speed/pagespeed/module` is described as tool that:

> *"rewrit[es] web pages to reduce latency and bandwidth."*

To download and install `mod_pagespeed` for Debian/Ubuntu Linux, run the following two commands in your terminal:

```
$ sudo dpkg -i mod-pagespeed-*.deb
$ sudo apt-get -f install
```

To do the same but for CentOS/Fedora Linux, run the following two commands in your terminal:

```
$ sudo yum install at
$ sudo rpm -U mod-pagespeed-*.rpm
```

Once the module is installed and enabled, you can utilize any of its many filters in `/etc/apache2/mods-available/pagespeed.conf` for Debian/Ubuntu Linux and `/etc/httpd/conf.d/pagespeed.conf` for CentOS/Fedora Linux.

Support for Angular's HTML5 Mode Angular has a lesser known method of the $location service that facilitates the configuration of how your application interfaces with the URL. Setting html5Mode(true) results in a fundamental change in how Angular routes views based on the URL, most notably by removing #/ (the default Hash mode) from Angular's URL structure. Enabling html5Mode will also result in elevated numbers of 404 Errors if visitors attempt to navigate to deep linked content. This unwanted side effect is curable by configuring Apache to automate a redirection to /index.html anytime an unknown URL is attempted. Because /index.html bootstraps your Angular application, and subsequently all routes, it will interpret the URL accurately and serve the content your visitor intended.

 Please note that using $locationProvider.html5Mode(true) enables Angular to use the HTML5 History API instead of the default Hash mode. You can find out more by visiting https://docs.angularjs.org/guide/$location.

The angular-ui or ui-router repository's documentation on GitHub provides snippets to configure Apache (and other popular web server environments) to support the use of html5Mode in your Angular application. This is possible by adding a file to the root folder of your application called .htaccess. Adding a .htaccess file will allow you to configure your Apache environment on a site-by-site (or application-by-application) basis, providing more granular control over your environment. Put modestly, the following snippet rewrites all HTTP traffic back to /index.html if the URL does not contain #/ (the Hash). Because /index.html kicks off all subsequent routing, your visitor will be served their intended content. Take a look at the following line of commands:

```
<VirtualHost *:80>
    ServerName my-app

    DocumentRoot /path/to/app

    <Directory /path/to/app>
        RewriteEngine on

        # Don't rewrite files or directories
        RewriteCond %{REQUEST_FILENAME} -f [OR]
        RewriteCond %{REQUEST_FILENAME} -d
        RewriteRule ^ - [L]

        # Rewrite everything else to index.html
```

```
# to allow html5 state links
      RewriteRule ^ index.html [L]
   </Directory>
</VirtualHost>
```

Summary

Deploying Angular applications to Apache can be as simple or complicated as you prefer. In its simplest form, you can use a client that augments the process for you, resulting in a drag-and-drop interface. If speed is your primary concern (putting the "hot" in hot-fix), then the FTP command-line interface will likely be your weapon of choice. And if you don't mind some level of configuration, and you fancy automation, then auto-magically deploying your code from GitHub on each push is your calling. However you've decided to move your files from A to B, Apache is undoubtedly an environment that any Angular application can be proud to call home.

Coming up next, we will explore the Node.js server environment provided by the popular platform service provider, Heroku. Prepare to dive deep into the depth of Node.js with the goal of optimizing it to best serve your Angular application, using the tools provided by Heroku.

3
Deploying to Heroku

Heroku is one of a few cloud application-hosting services that enable developers to spin up and deploy to their own private Node.js servers at minimal cost and effort. Heroku's services go beyond application hosting, by also providing elastic scalability, databases, add-ons, and real-time monitoring tools. Prior to now, you have served and deployed your application to a local Node.js server and a remote Apache HTTP server. We will expand on this experience and knowledge by deploying to a remote Node.js server running in Heroku's cloud infrastructure. As you have learned, Angular and Node.js fit very well together because the stack empowers developers to write and deploy JavaScript on both, the client and server.

In this chapter, you will learn how to:

- Effectively use the Heroku Dashboard to control your application
- Deploy to Heroku using Git
- Connect to your Heroku environment over SSH
- Optimize Heroku's configuration for serving your AngularJS application
- Avoid some gotchas and pitfalls along the way

Setting up your Heroku environment

There are many different ways to leverage the services that Heroku's cloud offers. Working with a Node.js stack will be our weapon of choice for this deployment, and is in my opinion the best hosting environment for a complex Angular application.

Creating an account

Creating a free account on `Heroku.com` is a highly straightforward process. Begin by navigating to `www.Heroku.com` and clicking on the **Sign Up** button. You will be prompted for a valid e-mail address—proceed by entering your daily driver e-mail address. Heroku will then e-mail you a standard account verification e-mail. Once received, select the link within your account confirmation e-mail from Heroku. Now that your account has been created and confirmed, you will land at your Heroku Dashboard.

Heroku's dashboard

Heroku's Dashboard is how you will manage your application's deployment, dependencies, and resources within Heroku's larger cloud infrastructure. It is helpful to think of your Heroku environment as ancillary to a **Virtual Private Server** (**VPS**) in that your environment is private, and you are free to install mostly any software using root access (more on that in the upcoming *SSH access* section). However, it diverges from a traditional VPS, in that you are provided with preconfigured server-side stacks that suit common web application structures. These result in the ability to deploy, run, and manage applications written in Ruby, Node.js, Java, Python, Clojure, or Scala in only a few clicks or keystrokes, without the need to manage physical or virtual servers. Heroku's server stack automation model is a viable way for any web developer to further transition their skill set from exclusively frontend or backend to full-stack, by means of removing a lot of the pain-points typically involved in rolling-your-own cloud infrastructure. This empowerment is a direct factor in both, Heroku's positive developer experience, and in their success as a company. Gone are the days when developers concerned themselves with physical server resource constraints, backups, migrations, and so on, all thanks to infrastructure services such as Heroku and others. Take a look at the following Heroku Dashboard:

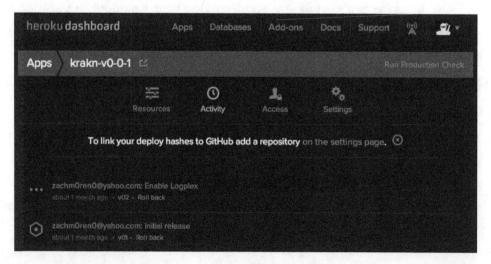

Defining a new application

Heroku provides two methods for interacting with your private cloud instance. The first is by using Heroku's Dashboard, while the second is by utilizing the Heroku Toolbelt command-line utility. The route you select to define your new application will not have implications on future deployments, nor management. My only advice on this decision is that if you have an existing app that is already somewhat developed and tracked by Git (such as krakn), the Heroku Toolbelt CLI will accommodate your existing workflow from the start, for reasons upcoming.

The Heroku Toolbelt

The Heroku Toolbelt is a command-line interface for interacting with the Heroku Platform API, responsible for facilitating all bidirectional interactions with a Heroku instance. Toolbelt is made up of a few open source projects (similar to how Yeoman augments sub-projects) that include the following:

- The Heroku client
- Foreman
- Git

As mentioned, the Heroku client interfaces with your Heroku cloud instance. While Foreman facilitates the use of **Procfile-based** applications locally (more on this in *The Procfile* section ahead), and Git is included because Heroku stores and interacts with all source code in the form of remote Git repositories.

Tasks that the Toolbelt facilitates include the following:

- Creating and renaming apps
- Recycling servers
- Running one-off dynos (more on that later)
- Capturing backups
- Configuring add-ons

Installation

To install the Heroku Toolbelt CLI, navigate to `https://toolbelt.heroku.com` and select the package that best fits your development environment's operating system (Windows, OS X, and Linux are all supported). Once fully installed, you may need to restart your terminal or command-line before the `heroku *` commands are available for usage. To verify that all `heroku` commands work as intended, run the following command:

```
$ heroku version
```

The output should read something similar to the following:

```
heroku-toolbelt/3.7.3.
```

SSH access

Accessing your Heroku cloud instance from the command line is simple, and is analogous in fashion to accessing GitHub, both using SSH as the transport protocol. Just as we created a public key for GitHub, we will need to create the same for Heroku. To begin the connection process, run the following command in your terminal:

```
$ heroku login
```

The output will guide you through the login and RSA key generation processes. You will notice that the Heroku Toolbelt provides a much more streamlined method as given in the following, for creating an RSA key when compared to the manual process we followed for SSH access to GitHub.

```
Enter your Heroku credentials.
Email: you@email.com
Password:
Could not find an existing public key.
Would you like to generate one? [Yn] Y
Generating new SSH public key.
Uploading ssh public key /Users/adam/.ssh/id_rsa.pub
```

 Auto update was added to the Toolbelt in Version 2.32.0. If you have an older version, please reinstall the Toolbelt using the instructions above.

New app in Toolbelt

With your connection fully set up, you are ready to create a new Heroku application using the Heroku Toolbelt—to do so, run the following commands in your terminal:

```
$ cd ~/Desktop/clones/krakn
$ heroku create
```

The preceding commands will create a new application within your Heroku cloud instance and create a remote Heroku Git repository, resulting in the following output:

```
Creating krakn... done, stack is cedar
http://krakn.herokuapp.com/  |   | Git remote heroku added
```

New app in dashboard

From your dashboard you have the facility to manage and configure all aspects of your hosted application, including resources, add-ons, activity logs, collaboration/access, custom domains, error pages, and more. Before the configuration optimization and tweaking begins, you must first define a new application. Begin by selecting **Create a new app** on your **Dashboard**'s homepage. You will be prompted to enter the name of your application, along with the geographic region you'd like to be hosted within; in our case let's go with krakn and the United States. The name you provide will then be used by Heroku to create your App URL and Git URL. Take a look at the following screenshot:

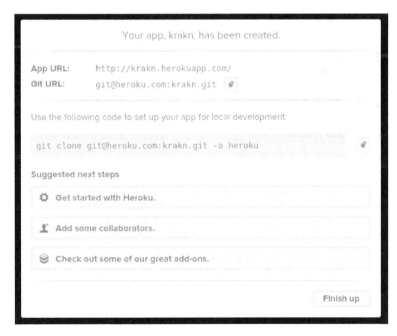

The **App URL** is what you might have expected, but the **Git URL** is why deploying to Heroku is such an enjoyable process. Below the two allocated URLs, there is a line of code you will use to set up your app for local development. The code is as follows:

```
$ git clone <your-git-repo-url>  -o heroku
```

The provided code essentially clones an empty remote repository (automatically initiated for you upon creating a new application within your dashboard) to your development environment that can later be pushed to your production application.

Do not run this command without first reading the following sections.

Heroku branch

Whether you have chosen to create your new application using the Heroku Dashboard or Heroku Toolbelt CLI, the provided command is not exactly what you need. As previously mentioned, the provided command will clone an empty repository, and because we already have code that is in need of deploying (krakn), we have little to no need for an empty repository. So the question then becomes, "how do we deploy our existing local Git repository, krakn, to the repository that has been created by Heroku?". The answer lies within Git branches. Currently, krakn has two branches that you have used: local master and remote master. The local master is basically your development branch, while the remote master branch is the single source of truth stored on GitHub (hence master). While the previous question is a valid concern, the solution is in fact, simple. We will modify the provided command to suit our needs, which in this case is to add the Heroku master repository as a new remote branch.

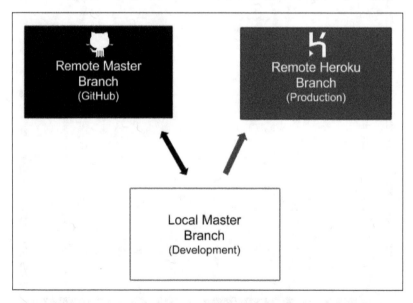

The preceding diagram illustrates how our desired branching scheme will work. All development and additions will originate from your **Local Master Branch**, these commits will be pushed and pulled from the **Remote Master Branch** on GitHub. The addition you will make is of the **Remote Heroku Branch** that was automatically created as a result of you creating a new application within your Heroku Dashboard. To achieve the above branch scheme, run the following commands within your terminal or command line:

```
$ cd ~/Desktop/clones/krakn
$ heroku git:remote -a krakn
```

Predeployment configuration

In the same way you configured your Apache HTTP server, it is valuable to configure your Node.js server before executing your deployment strategy. Some of the following enhancements and configurations are necessary for hosting an Angular application, and some are simply good form, but all are recommended. You will be adding some files to your application and examples of these files can be found in the /web-app subfolder within the krakn repository on GitHub.

Express

Express is described as a,

> *"minimal and flexible node.js web application framework, providing a robust set of features for building single and multi-page, and hybrid web applications."*

(Source: http://expressjs.com)

 There is an analogy I find useful when describing Express to potential or new users of Node.js and that is, "Express is to Node.js as Rails is to Ruby."

Node.js has no core notion of server-side MVC architecture, and Express fills that gap by providing a simple API for working with JavaScript on the server. It provides useful primitives for handling routes, requests, views, and more. For your purposes, you will be using Node and Express to serve your Angular application. Extensive knowledge on Express can be acquired by navigating to and reading expressjs. com/api.html.

Gzippo

Gzippo (pronounced g-zippo) is a gzip compression middleware for Express/Node.js applications that is developed and open sourced by Tom Gallacher. This will automatically compress all assets served to all clients that access your application, providing a stellar performance improvement to the already fierce speed of Node.js I/O.

Package.json

`Package.json` is the file used to configure a Node.js package. It is useful to view any application you intend on deploying to a Node.js server as a Node package, with `package.json` as the package metadata. The syntax will look familiar if you've ever worked with JSON (JavaScript Object Notation) previously. The `package.json` file has a defined set of keys that the NPM parser will accept, and therefore it is optimum to know the limits of what can and can't be done. At the very least you need to specify the application's name and version, as they are required for NPM to parse your `package.json` file. It is good form, however, to include the author, a description, dependencies, development environment dependencies, repository information, and license type. The following snippet is the contents of the `package.json` file you will find within the `krakn/heroku` directory on GitHub. Take note that the previously discussed Express.js and Gzippo are both included as dependencies of the krakn package, as these dependencies are needed to install within your Node.js server.

```
{
"name" : "krakn",
"version" : "0.0.1",
"author" : "Zachariah Moreno",
"description" : "Real-time chat application built atop AngularJS,
the Ionic Framework and Firebase for the book AngularJS Deployment
Essentials.",
"repository" :    {
"type" : "git",
"url" : https://github.com/zachmoreno/krakn
},
"license" : "MIT",
"dependencies" : {
"gzippo" : "~0.2.0",
"express" : "~4.2.0"
},
```

```
"devDependencies" : {
"gzippo" : "~0.2.0",
"express" : "~4.2.0"
}
}
```

For a full breakdown of all keys that NPM's `package.json` parser will accept, navigate to and read `npmjs.org/doc/files/package.json.html`.

The Procfile

As mentioned previously, Heroku runs applications in the cloud using an open source project called **Foreman**, a means of communicating a set of commands that will be run on your application's dynos (more on that in the upcoming *Scalability* section). Foreman does this by following:

> *"The Unix process model is a simple and powerful abstraction for running server-side programs. Applied to web apps, the process model gives us a unique way to think about dividing our workloads and scaling up over time. The Heroku Cedar stack uses the process model for web, worker, and all other types of dynos."*

When it comes to your desired stack, we only need to include a single command that instructs your Heroku application's dynos to run a Node.js server, while using the `web.js` file as Node's configuration. The command included in your Procfile reads as follows:

```
web: node web.js
```

With the use of Foreman comes a divergence in the tool used to serve your application locally, within your development environment. Up until this point, you have been running a local Node.js server by way of running the `grunt serve` command. Foreman is included as part of the Heroku Toolbelt, because Heroku's cloud uses Foreman in conjunction with your Procfile, to control the processes run on your environment's dynos. Your local Foreman is available by running the following commands within your terminal or command line:

```
$ cd ~/Desktop/clones/krakn
$ foreman start
18:06:23 web.1    | started with pid 47219
18:06:23 web.1    | => Awesome web application server output
```

When Foreman is run, it will replicate your remote Heroku environment on your local development environment. The level of precision is vital when developing features or fixes for a production application. The main consideration when making the decision to use `foreman start` over `grunt serve` is that the Node server provided by `grunt serve` will not run Express, Gzippo, or any other Node package unless configured otherwise. Aside from that concern, there is no reason why you can't continue local development using the Node.js server provided by the `grunt serve` command.

Web.js

So the Procfile is responsible for instructing your Heroku application environment to run a Node.js server, and you configure the Node.js server with the contents of a file named `web.js`. You defined the Express and Gzippo node packages as dependencies within your `package.json` file, now you will put them to work within your `web.js` file. The `express()` method is the namespace for all Express API calls, and you will use it here to create a new app and store log files within the Heroku development environment. Gzip and serve the application source code and assets from the `/dist` directory instead of the default root folder.

And lastly, start the Node.js server on either the default environmental HTTP port or port 5000 if one is not defined.

 Recall that Yeoman/Grunt place all optimized source code files and assets within the `/dist` folder, as a result of running the `grunt build` command. Without this configuration, your Grunt-built application would not run properly under Heroku's default setting.

Take a look at the following command lines:

```
var gzippo = require('gzippo');
var express = require('express');
var app = express();


// Store log files within the Heroku development environment

app.use(express.logger('dev'));
app.use(gzippo.staticGzip("" + __dirname + "/dist"));

// if you have html5mode enabled in Angular
app.use(function(req, res) {
  res.sendfile(__dirname + "/dist/index.html");
}


app.listen(process.env.PORT || 5000);
```

Scaling and deploying to Heroku

Now that you have a deeper understanding of how Heroku, Node.js, Express, Gzippo, the Procfile, and the `web.js` file all work together to serve your application, it is time to commence with deployment. Because Heroku stores all files as remote Git repositories, all that is needed to deploy code to your Heroku application environment, is a push. Simply run the following command in your terminal or command line to deploy your code to Heroku:

```
$ git push heroku master
```

This command works because the remote Git branch, `heroku`, was created for you when you created your application either in the Heroku Dashboard or Toolkit. At this point if you navigate to your application's Dashboard and view its activity, you will see a log of your deployment, along with the Git SHA-1 of your latest commit as confirmation.

Dynos

To understand how your Heroku environment can scale, it is valuable to first understand how Heroku measures your application. Heroku applies the notion of dynos as a unit of measurement for computing power. A single dyno is a single Unix sandbox, responsible for running a single process or command specified in your application's Procfile. Each new command you add to your application's Procfile will be run in its own dyno. Heroku's documentation best outlines the features of dynos as follows:

- **Elasticity & scale**: The number of dynos allocated for your app can be increased or decreased at any time.

- **Routing**: The router tracks the location of all running dynos with the web process type (web dynos) and routes HTTP traffic to them accordingly.

- **Dyno management**: Running dynos are monitored to make sure they continue running. Dynos that crash are removed and new dynos are launched to replace them.

- **Distribution and redundancy**: Dynos are distributed across an elastic execution environment. An app configured with two web dynos, for example, may end up with each web dyno running in a separate physical location. If infrastructure underlying one of those two dynos fails, the other stays up, and so does your site.

- **Isolation**: Every dyno is isolated in its own subvirtualized container, with many benefits for security, resource guarantees, and overall robustness.

Scalability

As noted in the Heroku documentation, dynos are elastic and scalable. This is achieved through the Foreman "process model (via [your] Procfile) that lets them scale up or down instantly from the command line or dashboard. Each app has a set of running dynos, managed by the dyno manager, which are known as its dyno formation." To scale the single dyno running your application from one to two dynos, run the following command within your terminal or command line:

```
$ heroku ps:scale web=2

Scaling web processes... done, now running 2
```

You can choose to specify the number of dynos you're scaling to, as an absolute value or as an incremental value, illustrated in the following command:

```
$ heroku ps:scale web+2

Scaling web processes... done, now running 4
```

> If at any point you'd like to ascertain all of the processes being run (dynos) by your Heroku environment, you can run the following command within your terminal or command line:
> ```
> $ heroku ps
> === web: `node web.js` web.1: up for 2m
> ```

Add-ons

Just as the rest of Heroku's features, add-ons can be managed from both, your Dashboard and Toolbelt. Heroku categorizes add-ons as either data stores, mobile, search, logging, e-mail and SMS, workers and queueing, analytics, caching, monitoring, media, utilities, and payments. Each category contains several add-ons that are designed to be as flexible as the rest of Heroku's infrastructure. For instance, it can be scaled, removed, upgraded, downgraded, and configured. Some add-ons provide a dashboard, such as the New Relic add-on that provides, "Monitor[ing], troubleshoot[ing], and tune[ing of] production web applications." To enable the use of an add-on, run the following command in your terminal or command line:

```
$ heroku addons:add newrelic:stark
```

The preceding commands provided in the heroku Toolbelt use the verbs you'd expect them to while interacting with your application's add-ons. Run the following command in your terminal or command line:

```
$ heroku addons:upgrade newrelic:wayne
$ heroku addons:downgrade newrelic: stark
```

```
$ heroku addons:open newrelic
Opening newrelic:stark for krakn.
$ heroku addons:remove newrelic:stark
```

> To list all add-ons currently being used by an application, run the following command in your terminal or command line:
> ```
> $ heroku addons
> newrelic:stark
> ```

It helps to conceptualize add-ons as backend services that improve your developer experience through aiding in application management, performance, and analysis. Some add-ons include a free tier, so there is little to no harm in experimenting with how you can improve your application by adding new backend services.

Troubleshooting deployment issues

Just as deployment issues can arise in deploying to Apache, mistakes can be made when deploying to Heroku. However, unlike Apache, Heroku's deployment model is based on Git's protocol and not FTP. While FTP is robust enough to facilitate deployments, it does not include the deep file analysis that Git does. This analysis is typically used for revision control and file diffing (comparisons), but it is also used when merging branches. And merging branches is exactly what you are doing when you push your code to Heroku.

> Recall that you conduct all development on your repository's local master branch and when you push to Heroku, you are merging your local master branch with your remote Heroku branch.

Because deploying to Heroku is simply a merge of Git branches, a summary of the changes made during deployment is provided as output to you, after the deployment has concluded. It is valuable to analyze this output to ensure that the changes you expected were made, nothing more and nothing less. In the event that unexpected changes were made, you can employ a previously covered tool to further investigate the discrepancy, the `git diff` command. For example, you just concluded running the `git push heroku master` command from within your local repository's master branch. Output of the changes is provided when concluded, and you notice that you forgot to add a dependency for use within a controller. The following command can be run to view the contents of the remote file in question:

```
$ git remote show heroku js/controllers.js
```

While this is nice, it is more useful to run the following command to compare your local `controller.js` from within its remote counterpart to ensure the mistake is what you expect:

```
$ git diff master heroku/master js/controller.js
```

The first parameter is the local branch name, the second is the remote branch name of the two you intend on comparing, while the third parameter is the specific file path/name. The same command can be run without a specific file name, and all files will be compared for you.

Summary

Deployment to Heroku's cloud infrastructure is a delightful experience that is both, empowering and fun. Heroku has developed an environment that has a number of qualities that make it a strong contender when choosing an infrastructure for your application or product. This is achieved by including the principles of redundancy, flexibility, and extensibility into every facet of Heroku. The notion of dynos affords developers the opportunity to exercise a granular control over their application's entire environment. In this chapter, we explored how to control your application from the Dashboard and Toolbelt, connect to your environment over SSH, deploy your application with Git, and optimize configuration for serving your Angular application, all while following the best practices.

In the next chapter, you will take your application to the new frontier of Firebase hosting. Firebase is an exciting company that provides a groundbreaking real-time data synchronization and storage service, and in May, 2014 announced that they are entering into the application hosting business as well.

4
Deploying to Firebase Hosting

Unlike Heroku, Amazon, or Google, Firebase has only been a major name in **Platforms as a Service (PaaS)** since 2013 and has only been offering hosting as a service since May 13, 2014. Age aside, the promise of hosting your application source code and static assets in the same environment as your real-time backend has created a lot of interest around Firebase. The Firebase team is 17 people strong, located at San Francisco, California and was recently purchased by Google in October, 2014. They have built a secure, reliable, and scalable service that syncs any application's data across clients in real time. While many applications offer the same syncing experience to their users via a custom API, these APIs are typically to some degree coupled with the applications they serve (custom methods, and so on.). Firebase disrupts this notion by allowing developers to create an API for their application in minutes that is in no way coupled with an application. The out-of-the-box functionality includes data storage, the **create, read, update, and delete (CRUD)** methods, the coveted bidirectional real-time syncing between the clients and server, and now hosting.

In this chapter, we will cover the following topics:

- Effective use of the Firebase Forge dashboard
- Managing application-specific security rules
- Simulating API requests and responses
- Leveraging the Firebase Simple Login authentication model
- Deploying your code and assets to Firebase Hosting
- Troubleshooting deployment issues

The Firebase setup

Analogously to Heroku, the majority of the services provided by Firebase are accessible through a web application located at `https://www.firebase.com`, while the remainder are accessible through the `firebase` command-line interface. Our journey begins by setting up your account on `firebase.com`.

Creating your Firebase account

To create your account with Firebase, we begin by navigating to `firebase.com`, and selecting the blue **SIGN UP** button on the right-hand side of the navigation bar. This action will prompt you to enter your desired e-mail address and password. Once these details are entered, select the blue **Create My Account** button (it is a good practice to first read the Terms of Service and Privacy Policy before agreeing to create the account). Once your account has been fully created, you will be able to navigate to your new Firebase Forge dashboard.

Using the Firebase Forge dashboard

The majority of the control that you will exercise over your Firebase hosted data and application will occur within the context of the Forge dashboard. Because you can host multiple applications within your Firebase account, you will first see the option **CREATE NEW APP** or to access the Forge of an existing application, as shown in the following screenshot:

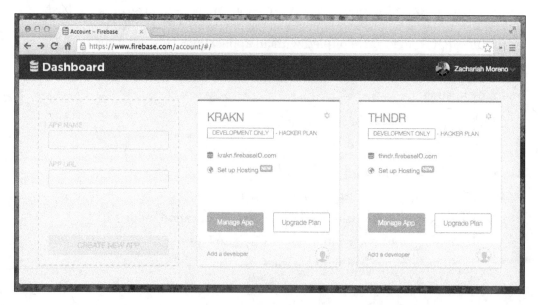

To create a backend for your application, start by entering the name of your application. Unless the name is already taken within Firebase, the App URL will default to `https://<your app name.firebaseIO.com`. After selecting the **CREATE NEW APP** button, you will be presented with a card similar to the two (middle and right) you see in the previous screenshot. To access an application's Forge dashboard, select the blue **Manage App** button near the bottom of the application's card.

Your application's Forge is organized into the **Data**, **Security Rules**, **Simulator**, **Analytics**, **Login & Auth**, **Hosting**, and **Secrets** navigation items on the left-hand side of the screen. The default, and likely most used, view is **Data**, as shown in the following screenshot in the next section.

Using the Data view

A few key interface elements to note within the **Data** view are the **Import JSON** and **Export JSON** buttons, the **Legend**, and the expandable tree structure of your data. All data stored and synced through Firebase is in the **JavaScript Object Notation (JSON)** format, and therefore JSON data can be imported and exported for quick access from within the **Data** view. The **Legend** is interesting because when data is **Changed**, **Added**, **Deleted**, or **Moved**, you will see the change take place in real time, and it will be color coded for quick visual reference. (You can literally watch as your visitors create and mutate data in real time.) Your data is displayed in an expandable tree structure to represent nested objects within your JSON schema. Individual values can be edited from within the **Data** view by clicking on the value; objects can also be added and deleted manually in the same fashion. Take a look at the following screenshot:

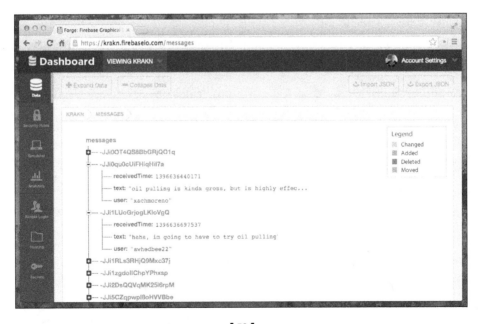

If you are reading this and were expecting to see a traditional SQL table view of your data, then now would be a good time to do a few Google searches for "NoSQL". JSON data stores are by definition NoSQL and therefore schema-less. This can be confusing (especially, because I just referenced krakn's schema) at first, because NoSQL does, in fact, end up having a schema; it is just defined in your application's source code rather than within the data store.

Using the Security Rules view

The **Security Rules** view contains a little more than a place to define the rules for how your data can be added or manipulated. Firebase have constructed their own JSON format for how these rules should be defined. The editor section of the view will validate the JSON structured rules and provide feedback in real time, making it fairly easy to write valid syntax. **Security Rules** in JSON are designed to follow the hierarchical structure of your application's JSON data. For example, you will specify all/wildcard rules at the top of the rules object with .read = false and .write = false, as given in the following code:

```
{
    "rules": {
        ".read": true,
        ".write": true
    }
}
```

The previous code snippet is the default **Security Rules** view that allows you to perform read/write operations on every nested object. It is important to note that once you change these values to false, you will need to specify the conditions when a client can read/write to an object. This is illustrated in the forthcoming screenshot.

The remainder of the rules are nested within the rules object and contain the rules for your top-level objects. In the following example, this pertains to the messages and users objects. The reason **Security Rules** are structured in this manner is straightforward; if a rule is defined at the top of the rules object, it will cascade down to its nested objects and apply to them, and if a rule is defined within a nested object, it will override the previous rule(s) and also cascade down to its nested objects and apply to them. This format allows highly expressive rules while allowing any level of granularity your application requires. In the following example, this cascading granular control is expressed by making all the data secure from the .read/.write operations, while these expressions are then overridden by the expressions within the messages object, where the .read/.write operations are, in fact, allowed. Beyond the .read/.write operations, validation can also be enforced by employing the .validate key.

In the following example, I am validating all of the nested objects written within a given message; this includes the text, user, receivedTime, and the catch-all $other objects. As each of these objects is unique and therefore requires explicit validation, the validation rules can be expressed as nested within each object. For example, the text object (the body of the chat message) validates that all the new data is a string that is less than or equal to 1,000 characters in length, while the receivedTime object validates that all the new data is a number. Take a look at the following screenshot:

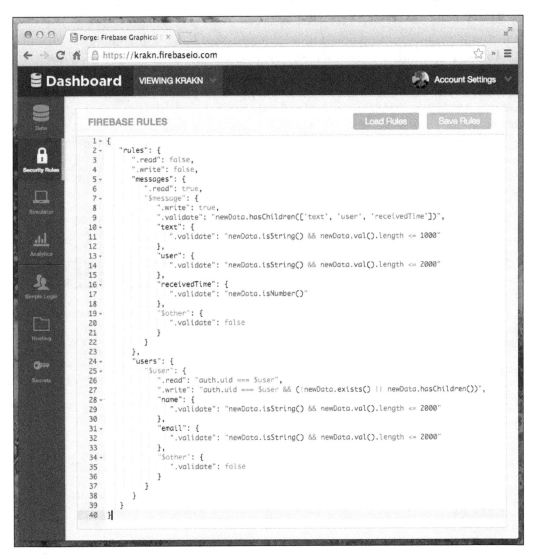

When you arrive at hosting your application, it is optional to specify your **Security Rules** view within the Forge dashboard or as a static file named `security-rules.json` that you host alongside the rest of your application. If you choose to host the `security-rules.json` files instead of defining them within the Forge dashboard, you will gain the added benefit of version control through Git, and you will still have access to them by selecting the blue **Load Rules** button on the top of the editing element.

Using the Simulator view

The **Simulator** view within your Forge dashboard provides you with the opportunity to simulate potential read/write operations before you begin developing your application. The simulator supports different levels of authentication along with the ability to attempt reading and writing to and from nested objects. In the following example, I am simulating an **Anonymous** user that is attempting to read data from the `/messages` object. Once simulated, the output is provided on the result of the simulation with the parameters I selected. The **Simulator** view is an excellent way to quickly test the security rules you've defined for an object at any level, and in this case, the read operation was allowed because of the security rules I have defined. Let's take a look at the following screenshot:

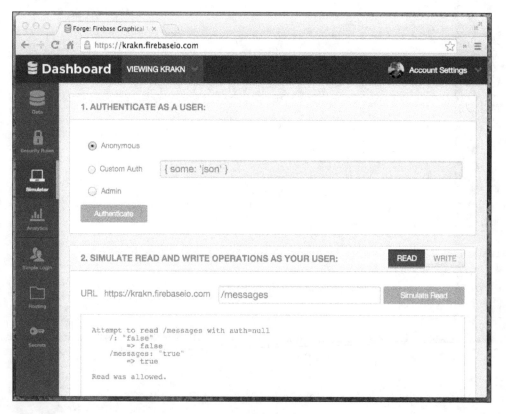

In the next example, I have altered the parameters to simulate a read operation from the /users object as an **Anonymous** user. Take a look at the following screenshot:

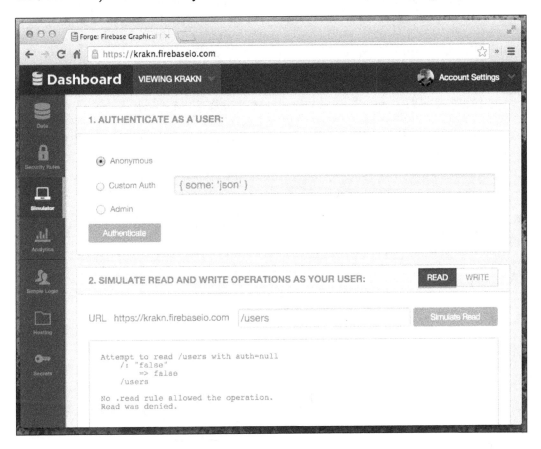

This result is denied as the simulation's output because a user can only read his/her own user data and an **Anonymous** user cannot read users' data this is also defined within the **Security Rules** view.

Using the Analytics view

The **Analytics** view is, as its name suggests, provides a snapshot of some key metrics along with a few data visualizations of **Bandwidth**, **Data Stored**, and **Concurrent Users**. Mainly, you'll want to monitor and be mindful of the amount of **Total Data Stored** to ensure that you are not exceeding the amount allotted for your particular storage plan with Firebase. Firebase has a similar pricing model to Amazon Web Services; in this, you are free to use and scale your services to your heart's/application's content, but you will eventually pay for it. In the following example, krakn only has **12.97 KB** of **TOTAL DATA STORED**, used **418.01 KB** of **BANDWIDTH** in the last 30 days, and had a peak of three concurrent users at one point in time. Take a look at the following screenshot:

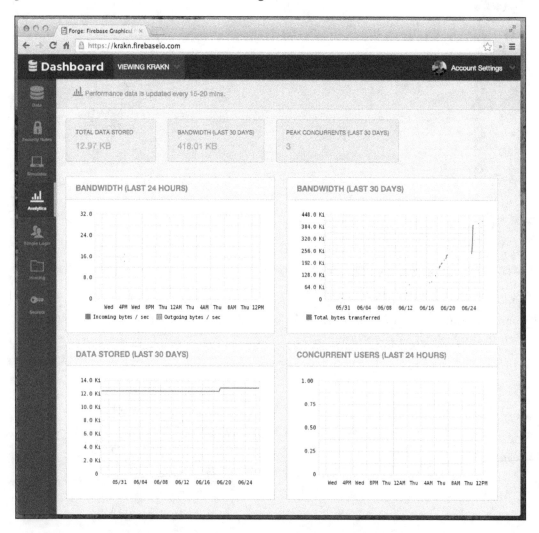

Using the Simple Login view

The **Simple Login** view within your application's Forge dashboard provides an easy-to-implement solution for your application's authentication model. You can specify **Authorized Request Origins** (client's or application's URLs) as an extra layer of security in addition to the previously mentioned **Security Rules**. Take a look at the following screenshot:

Firebase applications are all client side, therefore there is no "server" for you to define the length of a login session. This can be defined within the **Login Session Length** section within the Simple Login view, the default value being 24 hours.

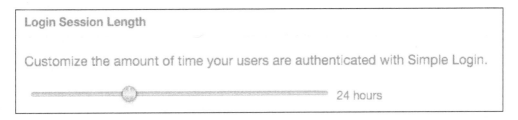

The bread and butter of the Firebase **Simple Login** solution is the ability to define a set of authentication providers through the **Open Authentication (OAuth)** standard protocol. OAuth provides a standard protocol for services to authenticate users with third-party service credentials instead of the user having to create yet another set of credentials, resulting in a better user experience. You have likely encountered OAuth in the wild, whether you realize it or not, as Google, Facebook, and Twitter have all embraced the OAuth standard, which means that other (typically smaller) services can authenticate users with their existing Google credentials. More information on the OAuth 2.0 standard can be attained by navigating to `http://oauth.net/`. Firebase **Simple Login** provides your application with a modest way to leverage OAuth from different services instead of rolling your own solution. Supported OAuth providers include **Facebook, Twitter, Google, Persona** (Mozilla Foundation), **Email & Password**, and **Anonymous**. I have opted for krakn to only support **Email & Password** authentication for the sake of simplicity, as all social providers require the attainment of an OAuth token and/or API key. By default, the **Anonymous** authentication provider is the only solution that is enabled, again for sake of simplicity.

For krakn, I have disabled the **Anonymous** provider and enabled the **Email & Password** provider, as in the following example. The **Email & Password** provider supports the ability to send **Password Reset Emails** with a default or customized email template. Take a look at the following screenshot:

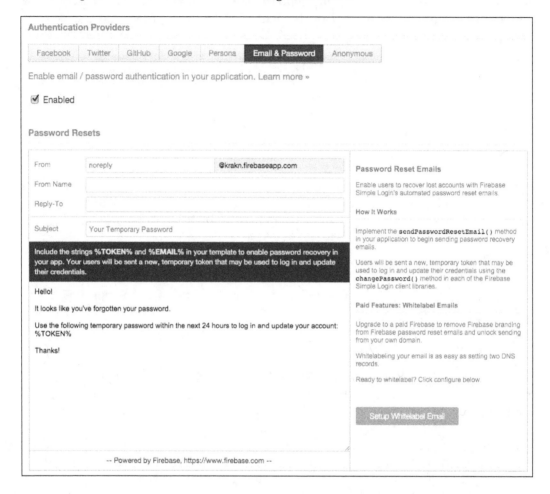

Lastly, a list of **Registered Users** is available to you with the options to **Delete**, **Create**, or manually **Send Password Reset Email**:

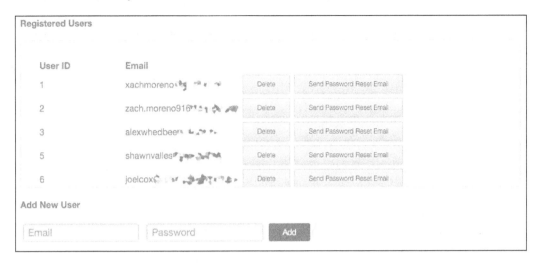

Hosting your application

Firebase Hosting contributes to your arsenal of environments that are easy to deploy Angular apps to. Features of the service include one-command deployment, SSL connections over HTTPS, domain customization, and content delivery for static assets. To work with and deploy it, you will need to employ the help of the firebase-tools command-line interface.

Using the firebase-tools CLI

To install the firebase-tools CLI, open your terminal or console and run the following command:

```
$ npm install -g firebase-tools
```

The preceding command will install the `firebase-tools` along with all of its dependencies using the same Node Package Manager that we discussed in *Chapter 1, Our App and Tool Stack*.

Configuring your Firebase environment

Your Firebase hosted environment is configurable via a file that you will need to create named `firebase.json`. The following command will create the `firebase.json` file by asking you a few questions, such as your application's name (the same as your Firebase backend), so in my case, it would be krakn:

```
$ cd /Desktop/clones/krakn
$ firebase init
```

The created configuration file is then populated with the following JSON:

```
{
  // required & name of backend
  "firebase": "krakn",

  // required & subfolder containing your production app
  "public": "dist",

  // optional instead of Forge => Security Rules
  "rules": " security-rules.json",

  // optional
  "ignore": [
    "firebase.json",
    ".*",
    "**/node_modules/**"
  ]
}
```

Now that your application is bootstrapped for hosting on Firebase, you can deploy it to production by running the following command:

```
$ firebase deploy -m "your optional message"
```

At this point, you can return to your application's Forge dashboard, and within the **Hosting** view, you will now see a log on deployment instead of the default instructions to install the firebase-tools CLI. The following example illustrates the UI controls provided within the **Hosting** view; these include the newly created URL for your app, a button to **Use a Custom Domain**, **Deployment History**, and a button to **Roll back**. Take a look at the following screenshot:

```
=================>  |   zach @ rinzler
| $ firebase init
Please sign into your Firebase account to continue...
Email: xachmoreno@gmail.com
Password:
------------------------------------------------------------
Your Firebase Apps xachmoreno@gmail.com
------------------------------------------------------------
krakn
thndr
------------------------------------------------------------
Enter the name of the Firebase app you would like to use for hosting
Firebase app: krakn
------------------------------------------------------------
Site URL: https://krakn.firebaseapp.com
------------------------------------------------------------
Enter the name of your app's public directory.
(usually where you store your index.html file)
Public Directory: (current directory)
Initializing app into current directory...
Writing firebase.json settings file...
Successfully initialized app
To deploy: firebase deploy
```

Now that your app has been configured properly with the creation of the
`firebase.json` file, you are free to run $ `firebase deploy`. Take a look at the
following screenshot:

```
=================>  |   zach @ rinzler
| $ firebase deploy
Preparing to deploy Public Directory...
progress: 100%

Successfully deployed
Site URL: https://krakn.firebaseapp.com, or use firebase open
Hosting Dashboard: https://firebase.com/account then view the hosting section of
 your app
=================>  |   zach @ rinzler
| $ firebase open
```

Troubleshooting deployment issues

As with the environments we have previously deployed to, deployment issues will
eventually arise. To ensure that they don't completely ruin your day, it is best to
research common pitfalls that could cause issues in your Firebase hosted application.

HTTP resources served over HTTPS

As part of the Firebase **Hosting** service, all the traffic is automatically served over SSL/HTTPS. Make no mistake, this is a positive statement, but it could potentially cause issues in the form of blocked content from external resources that are served over standard HTTP. I've run into this issue when deploying an application that still has resources loaded from a **Content Delivery Network (CDN)** that isn't using HTTPS. For example, navigating to `http://code.ionicframework.com/*` causes an error within the Firebase environment. Thankfully, the solution is straightforward enough. You simply have to replace the external resource call with either a resource loaded over HTTPS (most CDNs provide this service), or load the resource from within the same environment. So, instead of loading `ionic.min.css` from the Ionic Framework's (see *Chapter 1, Our App and Tool Stack*) CDN, `http://code.ionicframework.com`, you will include the file within your production code and run the following command:

```
$ firebase deploy -m "Fixed HTTP resource issue"
```

Once the issue has been resolved, you can view a log of your hosting interactions from within the **Hosting** view in your application's Forge dashboard, as shown in the following screenshot:

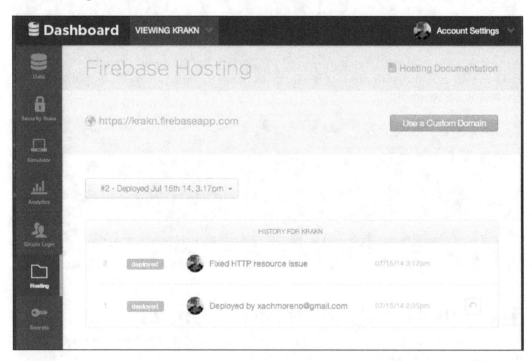

Summary

Firebase have earned a spot as a top contender in the platform as a service arena because they are arguably providing the best developer experience when compared to the services we covered this far. They provide a similar experience to Heroku, but with a number of improvements out of the box, including HTTPS by default and optimized content delivery. Moreover, I get a warm fuzzy feeling when I know that my application code, API logic, and data can all be managed from one location—Firebase's Forge Dashboard. It is clear that developers around the world have noticed Firebase and have begun using their services within production applications. For example, a few days before Google IO 2014, Nest announced that their device APIs are built atop Firebase. In my mind, this is a huge vote of confidence in the service from some of the top companies today.

In the next chapter, you will learn how to deploy your AngularJS application as a mobile app packaged using Apache Cordova.

5
Deploying a Mobile App

Web development has traditionally been discussed in the context of desktop web browsers, until recent technological developments that have given web applications a new contextual purpose. These new contexts arose in the form of quality browsers tailored to mobile and wearable devices. This alone was a huge leap forward for web applications, as they began to evolve to meet the needs presented by these new contexts. Many developers, and some users, still feel that web applications should be treated as first-class citizens on mobile devices with experiences that are on par with native mobile applications. This is the Holy Grail of the Web and its community because new contexts allow us to take our skills to new heights, and ultimately, provide the best experience possible, no matter what the context of use is. Most users do not care about what language their favorite applications or games are written in; all they care about is enjoying a delightful experience no matter what the device or context is. This is the reason open source projects such as Apache Cordova, Firefox OS, and Chrome OS were created to provide developers with new opportunities to reach and delight their users.

In this chapter, we will learn about the following:

- Emulating mobile operating systems within your development environment for rapid development and testing
- Packaging your Angular web application as a mobile application using Apache Cordova, Adobe PhoneGap Build, and the mobile Chrome apps tool chain
- Incorporating Cordova plugins to troubleshoot build/deployment issues on your physical devices
- Deploying your application to the Google Play Store

Context is the king

Most applications developed on top of a traditional web stack, including Angular, were designed with the assumption that the majority of users will access it from the context of a desktop web browser. This was the assumption made for many years until the iPhone was introduced on June 29, 2007 by Apple. The iPhone was the first truly "smart" phone, which means that it had a full-featured Safari web browser and other web service integrations. It seems that the term "game changer" was invented to honor products delivered by Apple, and the iPhone was no exception. Websites (and everybody else) at the time were seemingly taken by surprise, and the discussion on how to optimize existing websites for this new mobile device context began, a discussion that is still alive today.

Since 2007, we have learned from the trials, errors, and successes of web developers that have vetted out the pain points and best practices that we all should follow today. The Internet as a community and platform now support mobile device contexts by adapting layouts and styles to better support mobile form factors. These best practices provide a better user experience when compared to using a website only designed for the desktop context within a mobile context. However, when compared to native mobile applications, this seemingly improved experience steadily declines for the following reasons:

- No design/UI standards
- No access to native device APIs
- Limited sharing between web applications
- Added navigational steps to access

With the exception of the first reason, all of these concerns address the context in which your user accesses your application. Context is the king because the ability to provide the most relevant information at the right time and place (context) is a more positive experience for your user. These concerns, if left unaddressed, would always give an unfair advantage to native applications over web applications. Thankfully, the open source community has been hard at work addressing these exact concerns in the form of the Apache Cordova project.

What is Apache Cordova and how does it address issues?

The Apache Foundation's Cordova project is a tool that provides web developers with a means of packaging their entire web application with an extremely lightweight and "chromeless" web browser. The resulting package comes in the form of an

Android (`.apk`) or iOS (`.ipa`) file that can be manually installed on a mobile device or uploaded to an application marketplace for consumption by all of your users. The experience of using your Cordova-packaged application versus a native application is nearly identical. Because the operating system installed in the package is the same as a native application, users get an icon on their desktop to launch it, resolving the issue of added navigational steps to access. When the application launches, there is no URL input field nor home and back buttons (that is, a chromeless browser), so your application is viewed in fullscreen like most other native applications, addressing the issue of added navigation and non-standard design/UI. The final issues of no access to native device APIs and limited sharing between web applications are both addressed by the Cordova plugin system. Cordova plugins bridge the gap between device APIs and JavaScript APIs. Neither Angular nor vanilla JavaScript provide APIs to display OS-level notifications on your users' mobile device. Nevertheless, a lot of developers likely want to utilize this functionality in their Cordova-packaged web applications, and this is made possible through the Cordova plugin system. Cordova is smart enough to determine what device it is running on and how that device handles notifications, and translates the necessary device APIs into familiar JavaScript objects for use within your web application.

Configuring your development environment for Apache Cordova

Cordova, like the other tools we have covered so far, requires installation and configuration on your development workstation. Because Cordova is, in fact, dependent on a long list of other projects, I'll do my best to provide the most accurate information for the widest array of development environments. However, the truth remains that each of Cordova's dependencies requires differing instructions depending on your development workstation's OS. For example, Xcode can only be installed on an OS X workstation, so if you wish to package your Angular application for iOS, you will need to use a machine running OS X to do so. Conversely, if you are intending to deploy your application on Windows Phone, you can only do so from within a Windows environment.

 To my knowledge, the only way to get around this is to run a virtual machine with OS X installed as the image OS, and install Xcode within the VM. For further instructions on how to do so, navigate to `http://blog.getspool.com/79/download-install-xcode-windows-7-8-pc/`.

A word on Cordova's dependencies

I would be remiss if I told you that setting up your environment to package applications with Cordova is an easy process. It has a reputation of being difficult; however, the blame would be misguided if directed at Cordova. In my experience, the difficulties lie within Cordova's dependencies to properly install or configure the Android **Software Developer Kit** (**SDK**) and/or **Xcode**. Cordova is dependent on the Android SDK and/or Xcode because Cordova is only responsible for three-quarters of the magic that results in your packaged mobile application. The high-level process by which your application is packaged goes as follows:

1. You build your working mobile optimized web application.
2. You make sure that all assets and dependencies are included within your application's root folder (no external dependencies).
3. You run Cordova within your application's root folder and tell it whether it's destined for Android or iOS.
4. Cordova builds your application with a chromeless browser, icon, and other metadata.
5. Cordova hands the built application off to the Android SDK or Xcode and they package it as a `.apk` or `.ipa` file.

Step five is where the aforementioned difficulties lie. Nevertheless, developers have been working on this issue for a few years and the process is now less painful than ever, but I still hesitate to call it a positive developer experience.

Installing Apache Cordova

Cordova, like other tools that we have used for deployment, ships in the form of a **command-line interface** (**CLI**) that you will use in your terminal or a CMD application. To install this, you will again use the node package manager as follows.

```
$ sudo npm install -g cordova
```

> For the Cordova commands to be made available, you might need to restart your terminal or CMD application.

> The remaining dependencies that you will install are optional, depending on whether your application is destined for Android or iOS. If you are planning on packaging your application for Android, you will need to follow the instructions to install the Android SDK; conversely, if you are planning on packaging your application for iOS, you will need to follow the instructions to update XTools.

Installing the Android SDK

Before you install the Android SDK, it is a good practice to know what you are about to install on your (likely expensive) development workstation. The SDK provides you with the API libraries and developer tools necessary to build, test, and debug apps for Android.

Because Android applications are typically written in Java, the SDK ships them in the form of the Eclipse **Android Developer Tools** (**ADT**), Android Studio (Beta at the time of writing), and lastly, the SDK for an existing Java IDE. All of these three options will install the tools necessary to package your application as a .apk file that is ready to be installed on a physical device or emulator. The most stable of these options, and in my opinion, the easiest to install, is the Eclipse ADT. The Eclipse ADT comes with the following options:

- Eclipse + ADT plugin
- Android SDK tools
- Android platform tools
- A version of the Android platform
- A version of the Android system image for the emulator

For your purposes, the only factors that are of use are the SDK tools, platform tools, and emulator. Eclipse is just dead weight on your workstation and it's best to just let it be, unless you have aspirations of Java development. The SDK tools, platform tools, and emulator all need to be configured to work within your development environment. To begin, install the Eclipse IDE for your development workstation's OS available for download from http://developer.android.com/sdk.

> Make a note of the install location of the Eclipse IDE/ADT, as you will need it for future commands.

Once installed, you will need to configure the tools to work properly for use with Cordova.

Configuring the Android SDK and tools

Cordova is a CLI, and it is dependent on the Android SDK. If you guessed that the SDK is a set of CLIs used for working with Android, then you are correct. The commands do not necessarily work automatically within your terminal or command line. To facilitate this, you need to add the SDK tools and platform tools interfaces to your development environment's $PATH variable.

> Your development environment's $PATH variable is simply a list of commands that have been installed to work within your terminal or command-line applications.

OS X configuration

To add the two CLIs necessary for Cordova on OS X, open your `.bash_profile` file using the following command:

```
$ open ~/.bash_profile
```

This will open the file in your default text editor and allow you to add the following code below any existing code in the file:

```
# Adds android CLI to PATH variable
export PATH=${PATH}:/Applications/adt-bundle-<some-version-number> >sdk/tools:/Applications/adt-bundle-<some-version-number> /sdk/platform-tools
```

For the commands to fully work, you will need to refresh your $PATH by either closing and reopening your terminal or by running the following command:

```
$ source ~/.bash_profile
```

Windows configuration

The following screenshot shows the basic information of Windows OS:

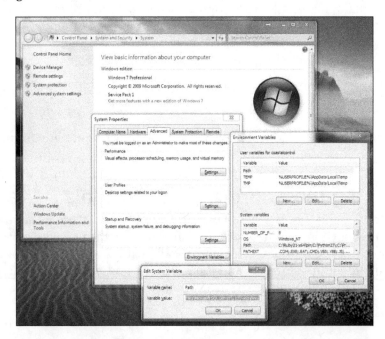

To add the two CLIs necessary for Cordova on Windows, begin by navigating to your desktop, right-click on **Computer**, and select **Properties**. Within the **Properties** dialogue box, select the **Advanced System Settings** menu item within the left column. Next, select the PATH variable from the **Environment Variables** section, and select the **Edit** button. Type the following code at the end of the provided textbox:

```
;C:\Development\adt-bundle-<some-version-number>\sdk\platform-
tools;C:\Development\adt-bundle-<some-version-number>\sdk\tools
```

This will add the two necessary Android CLIs to your PATH variable. Additionally, you need to add the following code (below the previous code) to ensure that JAVA and ANT are the available commands, both of which were installed with the Android SDK:

```
%JAVA_HOME%\bin
```

```
%ANT_HOME%\bin
```

Now, you can **Save** your edited PATH and safely close the **Environment Variables** dialog window.

> At this point, whether you are running OS X or Windows, you should be able to run the following commands with any output without an error output. If you receive the output similar to command not found, then revisit the previous instructions, rinse, and repeat until everything is configured correctly:
> ```
> $ android
> $ java
> $ ant
> ```

The most important of these commands is $ android, because it facilitates the installation and management of the available Android versions (also called targets) and emulators. To finalize your Android configuration, you will need to install the latest version of Android and create an emulator for it. Both will be used to test and package your application.

Installing an Android target and creating an emulator

To install the latest Android target, begin by launching **Android SDK Manager** by running the following command:

```
$ android
```

Android SDK Manager facilitates the installation and management of various Android targets (OS versions), documentation, tools, and emulators, as shown in the following screenshot:

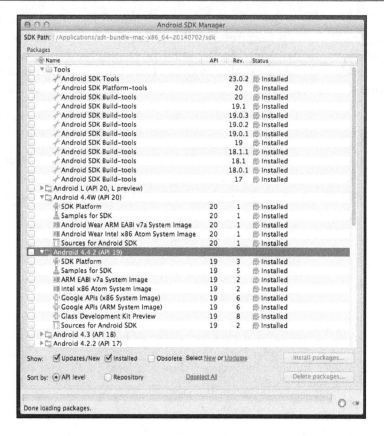

Cordova is expecting the latest stable Android target to be installed. In the list of Android targets, select the checkbox to the left of the two latest API versions, before clicking on the **Install packages** button (at the time of writing, I installed the API versions 19 and 20). You will need to read over and **Agree** to the requisite **Terms and Conditions** for each package before installation. Once the installation has finished, you can safely close the **Android SDK Manager** window.

To view a list of installed and available Android targets, run the following command at any time:

```
$ android
```

Now that the two latest Android targets are installed, you can create an emulator with them for testing your Cordova packaged application locally on your development workstation. To create your first emulator, run the following command within your terminal or command line:

```
$ android create avd -n <your-emulators-name> -t <your-android-target>
```

In my case, I named the emulator `target19emulator`, and I used `android-19` as my Android target. Take a look at the following screenshot:

When you run the previous command, you will often receive output similar to the following:

```
Valid ABIs: default/armeabi-v7a, default/x86
```

All this means is that there are multiple builds of the `android-19` target that you can choose from by appending some code to the previous command and rerunning it as follows:

```
$ android create avd -n <your-emulators-name> -t <your-android-target>
--abi <your-build-selection>
```

When asked, `"Do you wish to create a custom hardware profile [no]"`, hit the *Enter/Return* key and proceed without modification. With the successful installation of the latest Android targets and creation of a new emulator, you now have everything in place necessary to begin working with Cordova.

From Angular web applications to hybrid mobile apps with Cordova

With all the necessary tools installed, your environment configured, and your Angular application developed, you are all set to begin moving your Angular application from the browser to Android. To get the ball rolling with Cordova, you can run the following command from within the root folder of your Angular application's source code:

```
$ cordova create <subfolder-containing-all-cordova-code> <reverse-url-of-
app> <cordova-app-name>
```

I prefer to name the folder that will contain all the Cordova generated code/mobile app because it will contain all future mobile applications you intend to create such as iOS, Android, and so on. Because I followed this standard, my command was as follows:

```
================>    |    zach @ rinzler
| $ cordova create mobile-app com.firebaseapp.krakn krakn
Creating a new cordova project with name "krakn" and id "com.firebaseapp.krakn"
at location "/Users/rinzler/Desktop/prod-krakn/mobile-app"
================>    |    zach @ rinzler
| $ cd mobile-app
================>    |    zach @ rinzler
| $ pwd
/Users/rinzler/desktop/prod-krakn/mobile-app
```

Now that you have scaffolded the foundation of your future mobile application, you are free to add the platforms you'd like to package. To do so, run the following command:

```
$ cordova platform add android
```

The output is as shown in the following screenshot:

```
================>    |    zach @ rinzler
| $ cordova platform add android
Creating android project...
Creating Cordova project for the Android platform:
        Path: ../../../desktop/prod-krakn/mobile-app/platforms/android
        Package: com.firebaseapp.krakn
        Name: krakn
        Android target: android-19
Copying template files...
Running: android update project --subprojects --path "../../../desktop/prod-krak
n/mobile-app/platforms/android" --target android-19 --library "CordovaLib"
Resolved location of library project to: /Users/rinzler/Desktop/prod-krakn/mobil
e-app/platforms/android/CordovaLib
Updated and renamed default.properties to project.properties
Updated local.properties
No project name specified, using Activity name 'krakn'.
If you wish to change it, edit the first line of build.xml.
Added file ../../../desktop/prod-krakn/mobile-app/platforms/android/build.xml
Added file ../../../desktop/prod-krakn/mobile-app/platforms/android/proguard-pro
ject.txt
Updated project.properties
Updated local.properties
No project name specified, using project folder name 'CordovaLib'.
If you wish to change it, edit the first line of build.xml.
Added file ../../../desktop/prod-krakn/mobile-app/platforms/android/CordovaLib/b
uild.xml
Added file ../../../desktop/prod-krakn/mobile-app/platforms/android/CordovaLib/p
roguard-project.txt

Project successfully created.
```

I have touched on it before, but Cordova can package applications for various platforms, so you can run a similar command to add another mobile OS as a platform. If you are on a Mac OS X system, you are free to add the following platforms as build targets for your application:

```
$ cordova platform add android
$ cordova platform add ios
$ cordova platform add blackberry
```

Conversely, if you are on a Windows system, you are free to add the following platforms as build targets for your application:

```
$ cordova platform add wp7
$ cordova platform add wp8
$ cordova platform add android
$ cordova platform add blackberry
```

With each of these target platforms, there exists a unique installation and configuration process, which is similar to the steps you followed to install and configure Android. If you would like to do so, you can begin by running the `platform add` command for your desired target and following the instructions provided in the error output. They are typically very pithy and easy to follow.

> If you are picking up a project that includes Cordova, or inheriting one, you can run the following command to receive a list of added platforms as the output:
> ```
> $ cordova platforms ls
> ```
>
> To remove an added platform, you can run the following command with caution:
> ```
> $ cordova platform remove <platform-name>
> ```

Now that you've added Android, or another platform, you are free to take your newly created emulator for a spin on your development workstation.

Deploying your app to an emulator

Remember the Android emulator you created a few sections ago? Its primary facility is to provide you with a way to test your application within the Android OS environment without the need for a physical device. I think most web developers can agree that one of the contributing factors to a positive developer experience is a rapid development/test cycle. An emulator is not going to be as fast as a cycle or as fast as refreshing your browser, but it will be faster than loading the app onto a physical device every time you make a change to your code. To take your emulator for a spin and to see what is included by default, run the following command:

```
$ cordova emulate android
```

This command will take longer than (likely) anticipated to display your Android emulator, and then it will take another minute(s) to fully boot. While booting, the emulator will look similar to the following image. Patience is a virtue, and this is no exception.

Once the emulated device has fully booted, you can use the controls on the left-hand side along with your cursor to navigate the OS. To locate the Cordova application loaded onto the device, navigate to **Application Drawer**. You will see something similar to the following screenshot:

To open your Cordova-packaged application, click on the **Cordova** icon with the name of your application below it. Don't be alarmed when you do not see your application's interface; instead, you will see something similar to the following screenshot:

The reason why you are not seeing your application and instead see what is shown in the previous screenshot is because when you add a platform to your project, it does not automatically move over your source code. The reason being that you will likely have Cordova-specific code within your application's mobile version that you will not have (or want) in your original application source code. This is also the reason for placing all Cordova code and applications within a subfolder of your application's source code. At this point, you are free to close the emulator, so you can begin moving your code into Cordova.

Moving your code into /www

If you've taken a look through the folders and files generated by you, when `$ cordova create...` and `$ cordova platform add...` were run, you might have noticed the addition of a `/www` folder. This is where your mobile application's source code will live and be packaged from.

 Now is a great time to create a new Git branch for your Cordova-packaged application if you haven't already done so. Also, none of the `$ cordova` commands that follow are specific to Android and therefore all apply to iOS, Blackberry, and so on.

There's no shame in copying and pasting all of your web application's source code from the root folder into `/mobile-app/www/`. In fact, I'd like to start here and deal with errors if any. Now that your application code has replaced the default Cordova "Device is Ready" code with your Angular application's source code, it's time to rinse and repeat your Cordova build workflow:

1. Type $ `cd location/of/your/angular/app/mobile-app`.

2. Add $ `cordova build android`.

3. Add $ `cordova emulate android`.

   Allow time to fully boot the emulator.

4. Launch the application.

5. QA your application flow.

6. Make the following adjustments to the code if needed:

   $ cordova emulate

7. Build and reinstall the application within the running emulator.

8. Repeat steps 4-7 until the application has passed QA.

Take a look at the following screenshot:

To speed up your development workflow, you can "emulate" a device's dimensions, user agent, and network speed from within the Google Chrome Developer Tools. This can be useful if you make a small change and want to view the results quicker than emulating an OS. To do so, you'll need to launch a server within your /www folder by running $ cordova serve android and navigating to localhost:8000 from within Google Chrome. Next, launch the developer tools by typing *Ctrl + Shift + I* on Windows or *Cmd + Shift + I* on OS X. Finally, click on the mobile phone icon located near the top right-hand corner of the developer tools. Once the device mode has been enabled, you can select a predefined device (Nexus 5 is chosen, as shown in the following screenshot) and/or the network speed to quickly test your developments:

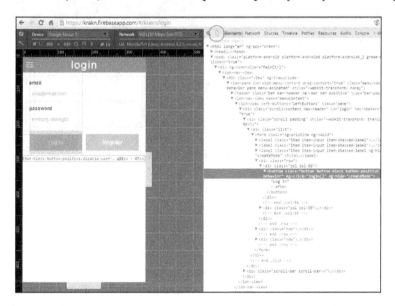

Deploying your app to your physical device with Cordova

You will likely quickly come to terms with the fact that all emulators, Android not excluded, are painful to deal with. It is also, I feel, much more gratifying to see and touch the fruits of your labor on your own device. However, Cordova gives you that warm feeling you get when using your own application on your own device. To do so, plug your phone into your development workstation via USB, and run the following command within your terminal or command line:

```
$ cordova run android
```

If you are deploying your application to your physical Android device for the first time, you must enable **USB Debugging** within your device's **Settings**. For more detailed instructions on how to set this up, go to developer.android.com/tools/device.html.

The aforementioned command does essentially the same things as the `emulate` command, but instead, it deploys your packaged Angular app to your connected physical device as an installed application. In the previous screenshot, I moved the app to my desktop for easy access and took a screen capture on the device (hold volume down + power to capture your screen on Android). Once you locate the installed application with your app drawer, feel free to launch it and QA its functionality, interface, and interactions. Similar to deploying and testing your application within an Android emulator, your workflow will be as follows:

1. Type $ `cd location/of/your/angular/app/mobile-app`.
2. Connect your physical Android device via USB.
3. Enable USB debugging.
4. Add $ `cordova run android`.

    Allow time to build the application and install it on a physical device.

5. QA your application flow.
6. Make adjustments to the code if needed.
7. Add $ `cordova run android`.

    This command builds and reinstalls the application on a physical device.

8. Repeat steps 4-7 until the application has passed QA.

Take a look at the following screenshot:

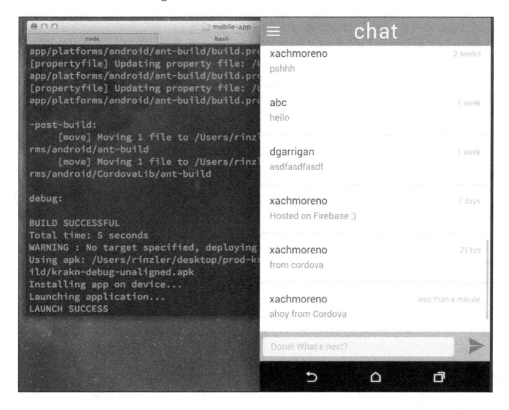

Now that your application has been tested both in an Android emulator and on a physical device by way of the `cordova emulate` and `run` commands, the time has come to explore alternate tool stacks that achieve the same outcome, but improve your developer experience.

From Angular web applications to mobile apps with the Cordova Chrome App toolchain

The Cordova Chrome App toolchain is the newest option in the web application to hybrid mobile app tool space, having only been released to the public in June 2014 at Google IO. It was therefore, at the time of this writing, still in the early developer preview.

(Source: `https://github.com/MobileChromeApps/mobile-chrome-apps`)

Because the Cordova Chrome App toolchain is still in the early developer preview (alpha), I was not able to successfully deploy krakn as a mobile app using the $ cca command-line tool. Nevertheless, the biggest complaint I hear from other web developers who have attempted to deploy a web application as a hybrid mobile application is that out-of-the-box Cordova uses the Android browser to display your application's UI. The Android browser is not to be confused with Google Chrome for Android, as the Android browser does not support nearly as many forthcoming APIs as Chrome does.

> Prior to Android v4.2, Cordova packaged app was shipped with an application called the Android browser, because a stable version of Google Chrome for Android did not exist. It was during this time that Cordova was created, and therefore Cordova still uses the Android browser application.

Now that Chrome for Android is very much stable and ships as the default browser on Android v4.2 and higher, we as developers want to leverage the forthcoming APIs and Chrome. Google's answer to this problem in the Cordova Chrome App toolchain, which extends Cordova, was to replace the browser it uses with Google Chrome for Android. Because it is built atop Cordova, your workflow will be strikingly similar.

Configuring your development environment for the Cordova Chrome App toolchain

To begin, you will need to install CCA, a command-line utility that will behave very much like the previously used $ cordova CLI. To do so, run the following commands in your terminal or command-line application:

```
$ curl -L https://raw.githubusercontent.com/creationix/nvm/master/
install.sh | sh
$ source ~/.bash_profile || source ~/.profile || source ~/.bashrc
$ nvm install 0.10
$ nvm alias default 0.10
$ sudo npm install -g cca
```

This will install the **Node Version Manager** (**NVM**) that allows you to use various versions of Node.js on your development environment along with $ cca.

Because the Cordova Chrome App toolchain extends Cordova, all of the dependencies you installed for the previous section are also needed for CCA. If you have skipped the *Configuring your development environment for Apache Cordova* section, please go back and follow the instructions given there.

Packaging your Angular web application for mobile with CCA

Because the CCA workflow is still in the early developer preview, the following will be an outline of the workflow in its current state. Before following the coming workflow, it would be wise to consult the current documentation for the project by navigating to `https://github.com/MobileChromeApps/mobile-chrome-apps/blob/master/docs/GettingStarted.md`:

1. Add $ `cca create YourApp`.
2. Move your Angular application's source code into the newly created `/YourApp/www/` folder (in the same fashion as Cordova):

    $ cca emulate Android

    This command will run your local Android emulator with your app installed for testing and QA:

    $ cca run Android

    This command will install your app on your attached Android device for testing and QA:

3. Optionally, add icons and/or a splash screen to your `mobile.manifest.json` file:

    $ cca prepare

    Run this command every time you make an update to your application to recompile.

While the Cordova Chrome App toolchain is a promising solution, it is still in need of community support and love before it becomes a production ready solution. Therefore, I encourage you to give it a try and provide any feedback you can to `https://github.com/MobileChromeApps/mobile-chrome-apps/issues`.

From Angular web applications to mobile apps with PhoneGap Build

PhoneGap Build is a cloud-based tool that achieves the same result as the Apache Cordova command-line utility without the setup. The key difference between Apache Cordova and PhoneGap Build is that Cordova runs on your development workstation, and therefore you are in charge of keeping all of your dependencies up to date and in good working order, while PhoneGap provides a cloud-based build environment and engineers at Adobe manage the environment for you. Apart from environmental management, PhoneGap provides a slightly different (some would say improved) developer experience through their web interface located at `https://build.phonegap.com/`. PhoneGap Build runs as a web application on a cloud infrastructure. The inherent improvements over running Cordova locally are as follows:

- Increased build speed
- Version and update management
- Cross-platform builds in one click
- No command line

To build and package your Angular application using the PhoneGap Build tool, we begin by navigating to the aforementioned URL and creating a free account. Once logged into your new account, you will want to create a new application by selecting the blue **+ new app** button. You will be presented with the option to either import your Angular app's source code from GitHub (if open source) or to upload your application as a `.zip` file. Choose the option that best works for your application, and upload it to PhoneGap. You will then be asked to give your app a name and optional description. The following step is the only configuration necessary to package your Angular application for mobile, which is fairly remarkable when compared to the setup for Cordova. You are now free to select the blue **Ready to Build** button to begin the cloud build process. You will see icons for each mobile platform with a loading bar below each that indicates when they have each successfully been built. Assuming that your platform(s) of choice have successfully built and packaged your hybrid mobile Angular application, you can install your new app by capturing a photo of the QR code on your mobile device.

 You will need a QR code reader application installed on your mobile device for the QR code to be translated into the application that can be downloaded from `build.phonegap.com`. Navigate to the App Store or Google Play Store and search for the QR code to install a QR code reader app on your device.

The following is a screenshot of the PhoneGap Build dashboard for the krakn application:

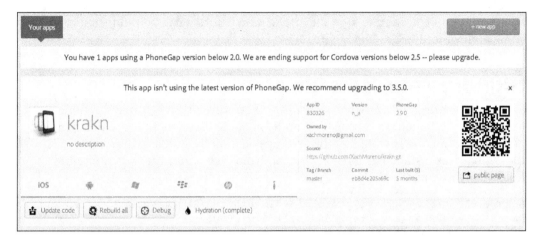

Publishing your application

There are a few steps you will likely want to undertake before publishing your application, such as including your icon and other application metadata that will be used when displaying your application on your chosen platform's application marketplace. To do this, you will need to modify the `config.xml` file located within your `location/of/your/angular/app/mobile-app/` folder to contain the following XML code:

```
<platform name="android">

<icon src="android/res/ldpi.png" density="ldpi" />

<icon src="android/res/mdpi.png" density="mdpi" />

<icon src="android/res/hdpi.png" density="hdpi" />

<icon src="android/res/xhdpi.png" density="xhdpi" />

</platform>
```

You will need to create these files, of course, and place them in the correct location as previously stated. Done correctly, from now on when, you run any of the `$ cca *` or `$ cordova *` commands, you will see the new icons on your device or emulator. Now that your application has been fully tested and has the marketplace metadata included, you can run the following command to output your coveted `.apk` file:

```
$ cordova build --release android
```

The generated `.apk` file can be found within your `bin` folder at `angular/app/mobile-app/platforms/android/bin/`, and will be named something similar to `<your-app-name>-release-unsigned.apk`. The `-unsigned` portion of the name means that you will need to sign the application before it can be published to the Google Play Store.

Signing your .apk file

To sign your unsigned `.apk` file, you will need to run it through an alignment utility to optimize its content for publishing on the Google Play Store. You will begin by generating a unique private key for your application by utilizing the keytool CLI utility that was installed as part of your Android Developer Kit by running the following command:

```
$ keytool -genkey -v -keystore android-signing-key.keystore -alias alias_
name -keyalg RSA -keysize 2048 -validity 10000
```

You will be prompted to provide a passphrase for the private key along with a few other questions you will need to answer. When the keytool is finished, you will have a new file called `android-signing-key.keystore` within your working directory.

 Make a note of both your private key's passphrase (necessary for encrypting your signed application) and file location, as you will need both for future releases of your application.

With your private key generated, you can now use it to sign your application using another CLI that comes with your ADK called `jarsigner` by running the following command:

```
$ jarsigner -verbose -sigalg SHA1withRSA -digestalg SHA1 -keystore
android-signing-key.keystore <your-app-name>-release-unsigned.apk alias_
name
```

Lastly, you will need to realign your `.apk` file to optimize it for publishing on the Google Play Store by running the following command:

```
$ zipalign -v 4 <your-app-name>-release-unsigned.apk <your-app-name>.apk
```

The result is the fruits of your labor so far — a fully signed and optimized `.apk` file that contains your Angular application package for Android by Apache Cordova.

Publishing to the Google Play Store

The Google Play Store, along with Android, has grown faster than any other mobile application marketplace since its inception in October 2008. This makes it an excellent platform for you to engage with new and existing users via your new Angular hybrid Android application. To publish an application to the Google Play Store, you will need to create a developer account by navigating to the Google Play Developer Console at `play.google.com/apps/publish/signup/`. You will be prompted to pay an annual $25 to register as a Google Play Developer, a fair price when compared to the annual $100 required by Apple's App Store. Assuming that you are now a registered Google Play Developer, you are free to publish your application to the Google Play Store by selecting the blue **Publish an Android App on Google Play** button, as seen in the following screenshot. Once selected, you will be prompted to upload your signed application, as you would upload any other file in a web browser. Take a look at the following screenshot:

Troubleshooting deployment issues

Cordova contains another valuable tool to help troubleshoot issues that can arise when setting up a new application or maintaining an existing application. It facilitates a quick way for you to check whether the code within your /www folder is not causing any JavaScript errors. To quickly check whether your Cordova-built application's code is sound, run the following command:

```
$ cordova serve android
```

The Cordova server will start a local testing server on port 8000 with the root being /www. You can then debug your Cordova-built application's source code like you would any other web application with the browser developer tools. The output in your terminal while the server is running is a list of HTTP traffic, which can also be used for troubleshooting if you are receiving 500 errors. Finally, to stop the server, type *Ctrl/Cmd + C*.

If your application is functioning as you intend within the local Cordova server, but not on your physical Android device, you might consider using a Cordova plugin called Cordova Console. To add this plugin to your development version of your application, run the following command:

```
$ cordova plugin add org.apache.cordova.console
```

The Cordova Console plugin will allow you to place traditional JavaScript `console.log()` method calls within your application's source code to output meaningful debug information when run on your device. Similarly, if you're feeling old school, you can place the `alert()` method calls in your source code to output the debug information in an alert dialog box.

Before running `$ cordova build --release android`, run the following command to remove the Cordova Console plugin in your production build:

```
$ cordova plugin remove org.apache.cordova.console
```

Furthermore, remove all the `console.log()` and `alert()` method calls to ensure the best possible user experience.

Summary

As you are well aware by the end of this chapter, deploying a mobile Angular application is a lengthy but rewarding process. Within the web developer community, the general sentiments around these types of applications is still mixed. Nevertheless, there are many developers working to improve the overall developer experience of deploying a web application to mobile. The most promising of which is Firefox OS, built from the ground up as a web-based operating system that runs nothing but web applications. This means that now, and in the not so distant future (in accelerated web time), web applications will likely be considered first-class citizens on the top of mobile platforms, Android and iOS (hopefully) included.

To conclude, you learned the brief history of how web applications came to mobile platforms, how to configure your development environment to facilitate the transition from Angular web to mobile app, how to use Apache Cordova and PhoneGap Build alike to package your Angular mobile application, and how to publish you application on the Google Play Store. I hope that this chapter has opened your eyes to the opportunities around building mobile Angular applications to engage with a wider audience.

Stay tuned, because next up you will learn how to deploy your Angular application as a packaged app for consumption on the Chrome Web Store.

6

Deploying as Chrome Apps

Google Chrome has succeeded and continues to succeed at its mission of *Moving the Web forward*, and Chrome Apps are just one of the facets of this success. Chrome is in the business of providing users and developers alike with the best experience possible. Your AngularJS application will soon be able to reach a whole new audience with Google Chrome as its platform.

In this chapter, you will learn how to:

- Configure your Chrome instance to test and troubleshoot your AngularJS Chrome App
- Augment your AngularJS application for packaging as a Chrome App
- Package your AngularJS application as a Chrome App
- Deploy your application to the Chrome Web Store

Why Chrome Apps?

Chrome Apps provide a unique opportunity to deploy your application in the same context as a traditional desktop application. Analogous to how Apache Cordova allows you to deploy your AngularJS application in the context of a traditional mobile application, Chrome Apps do the same, but in the context of the desktop. This is achieved by mimicking the user experience of traditional desktop applications and applying these standards to web applications. Because of these standards, users expect to access your web applications through their favorite browser, and conversely they expect to access their desktop applications by launching them from their OS's provided means (**Start** | **All Programs** on Windows and the `Applications` folder on Mac). Beyond location and means of launching the application, another key difference is that the desktop applications typically open in their own self-contained window. Chrome apps mimic this standard by providing an API for developers to express how their application should behave in this new context. We will explore these new APIs by deploying the krakn application as an AngularJS Chrome App.

Choosing the best app type

There are multiple options to consider before deploying your Angular application as a Chrome App. Thankfully, the Chrome team has recently released a decision flow chart that can aid you in expressing how your application will manifest within Chrome. The following chart also helps you distinguish between the app types by how your application will look and be used:

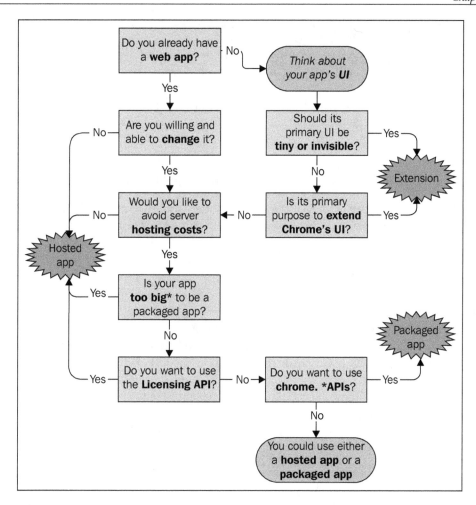

Because you are approaching Chrome Apps from the perspective of already having an AngularJS application built (or aspirations of such), the only choice you will have to make is between the hosted app type and the packaged app type. The biggest advantage is the 2 GB package size limitation. If this is exceeded, you have little choice and should move forward with a hosted app.

The Chrome App setup

Compared to the previous environments that you explored deploying your Angular application to, Chrome has a very minimal setup that requires almost zero configuration. To begin with, you should have the latest version of Google Chrome installed on your development workstation's OS. If you have yet to install Google Chrome, you can navigate to `http://BleedingEdgeBrowsers.com` to install the latest build.

 If you plan on using any of the `chrome.experimental.*` APIs in your application, you should have either Chrome Canary or Chrome Dev installed to ensure support. You can enable experimental APIs by navigating to `chrome://flags`.

Beyond installing, you will need to configure Chrome to accept local/unpackaged extensions for testing your Angular Chrome App. There are two ways to achieve your desired configuration. The first (and the fastest option) is to launch your Chrome browser and navigate to `chrome://extensions`. The second way is to again launch your Chrome browser, navigate to, and select the hamburger menu icon. From the drop-down menu, select the **Settings** menu item near the bottom. From the **Settings** view, select the **Extensions** menu item to the left of the view. Now all that remains is to select the checkbox that is labeled **Developer Mode**. With **Developer Mode** enabled, you will notice the addition of three buttons above your list of installed **Extensions**. The following screenshot illustrates that **Developer Mode** is indeed enabled, and the **Load unpacked extension...**, **Pack extension...**, and **Update extensions now** buttons are visible:

The key take away here is that you told Chrome that you will be testing either an extension or a Chrome App within your local instance, and Chrome said, "Great, here are some tools you'll need to do this." You will use these tools to test your Angular Chrome App locally and eventually to package your Angular Chrome App for deployment on the Chrome Web Store.

Augmenting your Angular App for Chrome

Now that Chrome is helping you with testing and packaging your application, all that's left to do is to augment your existing Angular application to support the Chrome App APIs and structure. When you **Load [an] unpackaged extension...** or an application into Chrome for testing, it is expecting to see an important file that tells Chrome how your application will work. This file is called `manifest.json`.

The manifest.json file

The `manifest.json` file is a simple JSON file that contains information used by Chrome to manifest your Angular Chrome App. The required keys that Chrome needs to successfully display your app include `manifest_version`, `name`, and `version`. The minimal syntax included in any application's `manifest.json` file is as follows:

```
{
    "name" : "app name",
    "version" : "0.1",
    "manifest_version" : 2
}
```

Icons

In addition to the required keys, you will likely want to include several keys in your application's `manifest.json` file, icons being one of them. Chrome is expecting specific sized icons to display your application on the users' computers and in the Chrome Web Store. The image sizes are 16 px x 16 px, 48 px x 48 px, and 128 px x 128 px. To include the icons in your `manifest.json` file, append the following syntax below the `manifest_version` file:

```
"icons" : {
    "16" : "icons/icon_16.png",
    "48" : "icons/icon_48.png",
    "128" : "icons/icon_128.png"
}
```

Content security policy

If your Angular application is like krakn and leverages Firebase as your backend solution, and you are using the Firebase Simple Login API, you need to be aware of Chrome's **Content Security Policy (CSP)**. The CSP does not allow your application to load external scripts or external object resources. As krakn's `module.SimpleLoginTools.js` file does exactly what CSP does, krakn will not connect to Firebase, as shown in the following screenshot, and therefore will not run as a Chrome App:

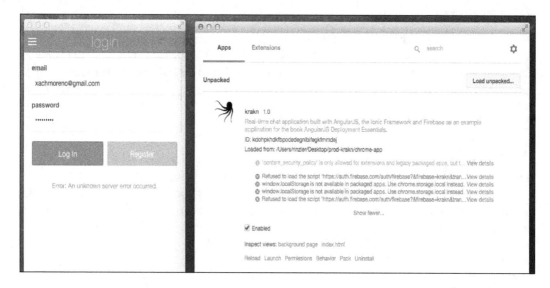

The CSP states nothing against the use of AngularJS, so it is perfectly legitimate to continue deploying your Angular application as a Chrome App. The Chrome App CSP is synthesized in the following points:

> *"You can't use inline scripting in your Chrome App pages. The restriction bans both <script> blocks and event handlers (<button onclick="...">).*
>
> *You can't reference any external resources in any of your app files (except for video and audio resources). You can't embed external resources in an iframe.*
>
> *You can't use string-to-JavaScript methods like eval() and new Function()."*

You can refer to Chrome's App policy at `https://developer.chrome.com/apps/contentSecurityPolicy`.

Other ways to customize your manifest.json file

Common additional properties are available to customize your application's `manifest.json` file, which are as follows:

```
"default_locale" : "en",
"description" : "A plain text description",
"browser_action": {...},
"page_action": {...},
"author": "Your Name",
"minimum_chrome_version": "versionString",
"offline_enabled": true,
"permissions": [...],
```

For a full list of available keys, you can navigate to `https://developer.chrome.com/extensions/manifest`.

`Permissions`, `offline_enabled`, `author`, and `description` are all used to optimally display your applications within the Chrome Web Store, so it is advantageous to include these keys in your manifest. You need to include a reference in your manifest to a `background.js` file. You will use this file to create a self-contained window for your application to launch within, achieving the same user experience as a desktop application.

The background.js file

You can name your background files whatever you like, but `background.js` seems to be the standard. The minimum code that you should include in your background file is the following snippet, and no Angular-specific code is needed within this file. `Background.js` is used by Chrome to manifest and appropriately size your Chrome-packaged Angular app's window. First, we will listen for the application launch event and provide it with a callback function that will handle your application's reaction to the launch event:

```
chrome.app.runtime.onLaunched.addListener(function() {
```

On launching, you need to specify that your application should open in a self-contained window with `index.html` as the initializer of your application:

```
chrome.app.window.create('index.html', {
```

You are free to customize the bounds of your application window with the following code:

```
    id: 'appWindow',
    bounds: {
        width: 200,
        height: 650,
        left: 100,
        top: 100
    },
    minWidth: 200,
    minHeight: 650
  });
});
```

Deploying to your Chrome instance

With the addition of the Chrome App-specific files, your AngularJS application is ready for deployment to your local Chrome instance. To do so, launch your local Google Chrome instance (the same one that you configured for **Developer mode**). You can now navigate back to chrome://extensions, and select the **Load unpacked extension...** button near the top of the page to the left. You will then be prompted to upload your unpacked extension to Chrome.

 You don't need to zip the root folder before completing this step.

Once it is selected and uploaded, you should be able to see the addition of your Chrome App within the list of installed extensions and apps. You might have also noticed that the name, version, author description, and so on have all been displayed, courtesy of your manifest.json file. Now that you have deployed your AngularJS Chrome App to your local Chrome instance, you can navigate to chrome://apps, and you should see your application's icon and name within the list of installed Chrome Apps, as shown in the following screenshot:

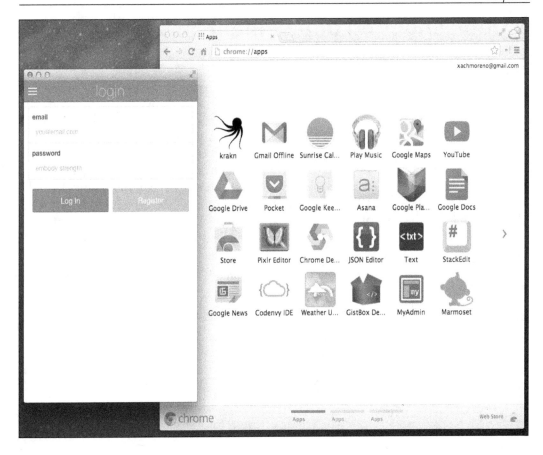

Note that your icon and name are both used in this interface, and that your application should have been launched in the size/bounds that you specified in your `background.js` file. If you find the need to update your application's source code, `manifest.json` file, or `background.js` file, you will need to return to the `chrome://extensions` page, and click on the **Update extensions now** button near the top of the page to the right. This will automatically pull in the latest changes to your installed AngularJS Chrome App.

Troubleshooting deployment issues

If, like me, you are experiencing deployment issues with your AngularJS Chrome App, take comfort in the fact that the Chrome Developer Tools can be used to the same effect as on a normal hosted web application or site. Before the Chrome DevTools are needed, you will likely see an error just below your application on the `chrome://extensions` page right after you upload your application to your local Chrome instance. If so, navigate to `chrome://apps` and proceed with launching your application. Now, you can inspect the damaged code by navigating to `chrome://inspect` and navigating to the Apps list from the left-hand side menu. You should be able to see your application listed within the Apps with a link below it that is labeled **inspect**, as shown in the following screenshot. To launch **DevTools**, click on the link. The best place to start within the **DevTools** page is the **Console** panel, which is like any other JavaScript console and it will give you any detailed error messages. It is worth noting that you can use the other **DevTools** panel to the same effect as on any other hosted web application or site, including performance **audits**, **timeline**, and **network**.

Deploying to the Chrome Web Store

Deploying to the Chrome Web Store is very similar to the process you followed in the previous chapter of deploying to the Google Play Store with your AngularJS Hybrid Android application. To begin with, you will need to zip your AngularJS Chrome App, which you will soon upload to the Chrome Web Store Developer Dashboard. Once it is zipped, navigate to `https://chrome.google.com/webstore/developer/dashboard`, and sign in with your Google account. When you are successfully authenticated into the Chrome Web Store Developer Dashboard, the only real action you can do is click on the **Add new item** on the right-hand side of the page. When you click on this tab, you will be prompted to upload the ZIP file of your AngularJS Chrome App that you created. Please do so:

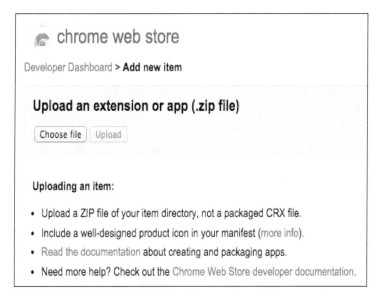

You will then be presented with a form to further customize how your Chrome App will be presented within the Chrome Web Store, such as a detailed description, screenshots, YouTube video, promo images, Analytics tracing code, websites, and more as follows:

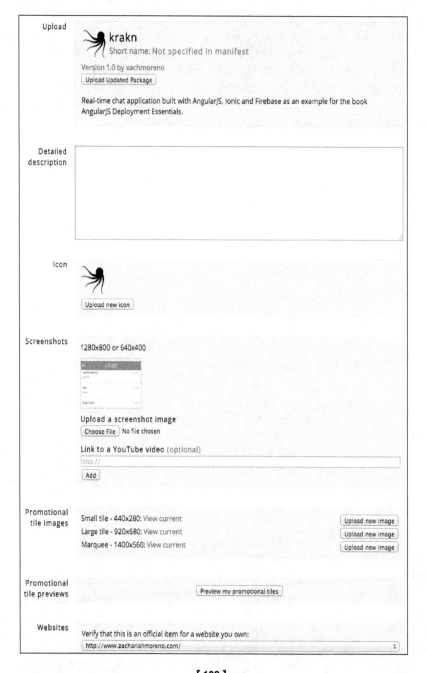

Apart from further promotional options, this page provides you with a tool for previewing your promotional tiles, as they will be presented within the Chrome Web Store. To utilize this tool, click on the **Preview my promotional tiles** button near the middle of the page. Your promotion tiles preview will look similar to the following screenshot:

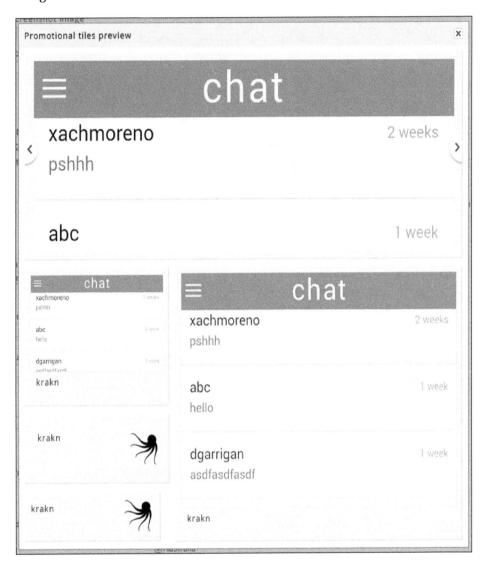

Now that you have fully customized your application's promotional experience all that remains to do is to select the **Publish application** button on the right-hand side of the page near the bottom of the form. You will be prompted to confirm the publishing action and redirected to your application within the live Chrome Web Store, which is similar to the following screenshot:

Congratulations! You just successfully deployed your AngularJS Chrome App to the Chrome Web Store for consumption by millions of users.

Summary

Compared to the other platforms and environments, the Google Chrome Web Store is the newest and most exciting. Android, the Chrome browser, and Chrome OS are all platforms for users to discover and engage with your AngularJS Chrome applications. It is exponentially powerful to build a single application that can be deployed to and thrive within such a diverse array of environments while maintaining your creative vision. To attain this power, you learned how to configure your Chrome instance to test and troubleshoot your AngularJS Chrome App. You then augmented your AngularJS application for packaging as a Chrome App and deployment to the Chrome Web Store. Lastly, you explored how to customize and polish your application to be presented within the Chrome Web Store to further enhance your users' experience.

In the next chapter, you will learn how to manage the postdeployment phase of your AngularJS application's life cycle. This includes application monitoring, analytics, deploying updates, and much more.

7
Postdeployment

Your strategy and workflows for postdeployment maintenance, fixes, and feature additions contribute in large part to how your application will be enjoyed by your users. Therefore, it is key to form and understand these workflows well before your begin shipping updates into production.

In this chapter, you will learn how to:

- Incorporate Google Analytics into your AngularJS application
- Confidently deploy updates to all of the environments we explored so far

Features and fixes

Updates typically fall into one of the two distinct categories: fixes and features. My wish for your Angular application is that you spend the majority of your time on features compared to fixes. However, when issues do arise, it is up to you to form a strategy before you are forced to deploy a hot fix into production. Your strategy for how you handle deploying fixes will contribute to your user perception and experience, and we all agree that perception is key.

Adding support to Google Analytics

Adding Google Analytics to a web application is typically a straightforward process. However, when you make the jump to a **Single Page Application** (**SPA**) framework, such as AngularJS, things get a little more complicated for Google Analytics. Because of Angular's ng-view directive (within your index.html) injecting content upon route changes, the tracking necessary for Google Analytics does not get updated upon such events. Luckily, Angular's community has stepped up to this challenge and produced a third-party module called angular-google-analytics that resolves the challenges faced in this endeavor. The angular-google-analytics module resolves our worries by providing a service that sends a new pageview event to Google Analytics whenever your Angular application's $location.path() changes.

Setting up the angular-google-analytics module

I'll assume that you already have a Google account with a Google Analytics site set up and ready to receive data. This means you should already have your tracking ID in hand, something such as UA-xxxxx-xx. Apart from this, all you need is your already installed Bower **command-line interface** (**CLI**).

We begin by opening your terminal or command-line application and navigating to the root of your Angular application, or the folder that contains your /bower_ components folder. To install the angular-google-analytics module along with its dependencies within your application, run the following command:

```
bower install angular-google-analytics –save
```

Next, you need to add a reference to the module's code within your index.html file (somewhere below your reference to AngularJS) as follows:

```
<script src="bower_components/angular-google-
    analytics/dist/angular-google-analytics.js></script>
```

Now, kindly switch over to your app.js file, the one that contains your global app definition, and add the following line of code to inject the angular-google-analytics module as a global dependency:

```
var app = angular.module('yourAppName',
  ['angular-google-analytics', … ])
```

All that remains to be done is to configure how you'd like to utilize Google Analytics within your AngularJS application. The bare minimum here is your previously attained Analytics tracking ID, an example of which is as follows:

```
.config(function(AnalyticsProvider) {
    // initial configuration
    AnalyticsProvider.setAccount('UA-XXXXX-xx');

    // optional track all routes (or not)
    AnalyticsProvider.trackPages(true);
}))

.run(function(Analytics) {
    // inject Analytics at least once within your application
    // to automatically track all routes
});
```

Another option that you have instead of injecting the `analytics` module as a dependency of the global `run()` method is to explicitly track individual pages at the controller level. The only difference with this setup is that there is an extra line of code per controller, but it's nice to have this level of granular control at your disposal. To leverage the `analytics` module at the controller level, first, inject the `analytics` module as a dependency of your controller, and then call the `Analytics.trackPage()` method with the only argument being the route you want to track as follows:

```
.controller('radController', ['Analytics', function(Analytics) {
    // create a new pageview event
    Analytics.trackPage('/your/rad/route');
    ...
}]);
```

The control you have over this module doesn't stop there. It can be configured to track any other event you find valuable, support cross-domain linking, and even to track e-commerce-specific events with the use of the `Analytics.addTrans()` method. If interested, you can navigate to `https://github.com/revolunet/angular-google-analytics` to look over the full documentation or possibly contribute to this effort.

Now that you have updated your AngularJS application with a useful enhancement, you can learn how to deploy the updates to all of the environments we have covered so far.

Deploying updates to Apache

In *Chapter 2, Deploying to Apache,* you learned how to configure your Apache environment to best serve your optimized AngularJS application. From this chapter, you learned how to deploy your Angular application from your local Apache environment to your remote Apache environment with the aid of FTP CLI and automated SSH. You will build on this knowledge by learning how to deploy updates to your production Apache server with both FTP and SSH.

The FTP command-line interface

Deploying an update to Apache from your terminal or command-line application is a highly straightforward process. All you need do is to perform the following steps:

1. Launch your terminal or command-line application as follows:

    ```
    $ cd path/to/your/local/apache/htdocs/app/dist
    $ ftp 123.4.5.678
    ftp> cd path/to/your/public_html/app
    ftp> mput *
    ftp> close
    ```

2. Confirm that the update was a success.

To recap the FTP deployment workflow; you need to navigate to your locally built AngularJS application, connect to your production Apache server over the FTP protocol, navigate to the root of your production application, push the entire folder from local to production, and finally, close the FTP connection.

An FTP client

An FTP client improves on the same deployment workflow by adding the ability to drag and drop your files into production.

1. Launch your FTP client (FileZilla, Transmit, and so on).
2. Navigate to your locally built copy of your application's source code on the left-hand side of the interface.
3. Connect to your production Apache server on the right-hand side of the interface.
4. Navigate to the root of your production Angular application.
5. Select the updated files/folders/resources on the left-hand side and drag them to the right.
6. Confirm that the update was a success.

Git and SSH

Deploying over the SSH protocol with `git push` is the most empowering means of deployment I have encountered. It encourages the following best practices in your workflow simply as a side effect of configuring your production server to accept the automated deployments:

1. Launch your terminal or command-line application as follows:

   ```
   $ cd path/to/your/local/apache/htdocs/app/dist
   $ git push origin master
   ```

2. Confirm that the update was a success.

To recap the SSH and Git deployment workflow, you navigated to your locally built AngularJS application and pushed your updated code to your application's GitHub repository. Remember that once an update is pushed to GitHub, a service hook is triggered that SSHes the updated code to your production environment.

Deploying updates to Heroku

In *Chapter 3*, *Deploying to Heroku*, you learned how to configure your Heroku environment to best serve your optimized AngularJS application. From this chapter, you learned how to deploy your Angular application from your local Node.js environment to your remote Heroku environment with the aid of the Heroku Toolbelt CLI. Deploying updates to Heroku is just a simple process as your Git and SSH workflow we just covered. The only difference is that the remote branch you're pushing to is not GitHub, but instead, your Heroku instance. You will build on this knowledge by learning how to deploy updates to your production Node.js server with the Heroku Toolbelt.

1. Launch your terminal or command-line application as follows:

   ```
   $ cd path/to/your/local/apache/htdocs/app/dist
   $ heroku login
   ```

2. Authenticate with your Heroku credentials as follows:

   ```
   $ git push heroku master
   $ heroku logout
   ```

3. Confirm that the update was a success.

To recap the Heroku deployment workflow, you navigated to your locally built AngularJS application and pushed your updated code to your production Heroku repository. To ensure the deployment was successful, log into your **Heroku Dashboard** and navigate to **Activity** to view a log of your deployments.

Deploying updates to Firebase Hosting

In *Chapter 4, Deploying to Firebase Hosting,* you learned how to utilize your Firebase Hosting environment to best serve your optimized AngularJS application. From this chapter, you learned how to deploy your Angular application from your local Node.js environment to your remote Firebase Hosting environment with the aid of the Firebase CLI. Deploying updates to your Firebase Hosting is just as simple a process as your Heroku workflow we just covered. The only difference is that the Firebase CLI facilitates the update push by way of the deploy command.

1. Launch your terminal or command-line application as follows:

   ```
   $ cd path/to/your/local/apache/htdocs/app/dist
   $ firebase login
   ```

2. Authenticate with your Firebase credentials as follows:

   ```
   $ firebase deploy -m "your update summary"
   $ firebase logout
   ```

3. Confirm that the update was a success.

To recap the Firebase deployment workflow, you navigated to your locally built AngularJS application and pushed your updated code to your Firebase Hosting production environment. To ensure the deployment was successful, log into your **Firebase Forge Dashboard** and navigate to **Hosting** to view a log of your deployments or to **Roll back** for the update.

Deploying updates to mobile apps

In *Chapter 5, Deploying a Mobile App,* you learned how to build your Angular application and package it as a hybrid mobile application with some additions to your tool-stack. From this chapter, you learned how to deploy your Angular hybrid application from your local development environment to the Google Play Store for consumption by millions. Deploying updates to your AngularJS hybrid application is an enjoyable process, because your environment has already undergone the necessary configuration covered in *Chapter 5, Deploying a Mobile App.* Recall that there is minimal differences in the workflows of Cordova and CCA because they are using the same underlying technology and swapping only the browser from the Android browser to Google Chrome.

Deploying updates to the local emulator with Cordova

Your local emulators are a quick-and-dirty way to test small to moderate changes to your hybrid application.

1. Launch your terminal or command-line application as follows:

```
$ cd path/to/your/angular/app/mobile-app
$ cordova build <platform>
$ cordova emulate <platform>
```

2. Launch the application.
3. Confirm that the update was a success.

To recap the Cordova deployment workflow, you navigated to your locally built AngularJS application, built the updated native application, installed it within an emulator, booted the emulator, and ensured that the update was successful.

Deploying updates to the physical device with Cordova

Installing your updated Angular hybrid application on the metal is essentially the same process as with the emulator, except the only difference is use of the run command instead of the build and emulate commands.

1. Connect your physical device to your development workstation via USB.
2. Enable **USB Debugging**.
3. Launch you terminal or command-line application as follows:

```
$ cd path/to/your/angular/app/mobile-app
$ cordova run <platform>
```

4. Launch the application.
5. Confirm that the update was a success.

Deploying updates to the local emulator with CCA

CCA enhances your hybrid application by providing a more capable run-time in Google Chrome for your Angular app.

1. Launch your terminal or command-line application as follows:

```
$ cd path/to/your/angular/app/mobile-app
$ cca build <platform>
$ cca emulate <platform>
```

2. Launch the application.
3. Confirm that the update was a success.

Deploying updates to the physical device with CCA

CCA can deploy your mobile hybrid Angular app to your physical device for a more real-world test environment in much the same way as Cordova does.

1. Connect your physical device to your development workstation via USB.
2. Enable **USB Debugging**.
3. Launch your terminal or command-line application as follows:

   ```
   $ cd path/to/your/angular/app/mobile-app
   $ cca run <platform>
   ```

4. Launch the application.
5. Confirm that the update was a success.

Building updates with PhoneGap Build

PhoneGap Build makes building an updated version of your Angular hybrid app as simple as clicking on a button and uploading a file. It's a remarkable feat when compared to building your app for each platform manually.

1. Zip up your updated and built application.
2. Navigate to http://build.phonegap.com/.
3. Authenticate with your GitHub credentials.
4. Select the **Update Code** button under your application.
5. Upload the updated .zip file when prompted.
6. Watch PhoneGap building your application for each platform.
7. Install the update on your physical device with the provided QR code.
8. Confirm that the update was a success.

Deploying updates to Google Play Store

The fruits of your labor are realized once you publish your updated application to the Google Play Store or Apple App Store, and this too is as simple as clicking on a button and uploading a file.

1. Attain your Cordova, CCA, or PhoneGap built .apk file for your updated Angular hybrid application.
2. Navigate to https://play.google.com/apps/publish.
3. Authenticate with your Google Account.
4. Navigate to the **APK** tab.

5. Select the **Upload new APK to Production** button.

6. Select your updated and built .apk file and upload.

7. Select the **Publish** button.

8. Install the update on your physical device from your application's Play Store listing.

9. Confirm that the update was a success.

Deploying updates to Chrome App

In *Chapter 6, Deploying as Chrome Apps,* you learned how to augment and package your Angular application as a Chrome App with the help of your local Google Chrome instance. From this chapter, you learned how to deploy your Angular Chrome App from your local Chrome instance to the Chrome Web Store for consumption by millions.

Packing updates with your local Chrome instance

To package an updated version of your Angular Chrome app, repeat the Pack Extension process that we covered in *Chapter 6, Deploying as Chrome Apps,* but with your updated application.

1. Launch Google Chrome.

2. Navigate to chrome://extensions.

3. Select the **Update extensions now** button to the upper-right of the view.

4. Launch a new tab.

5. Navigate to chrome://apps.

6. Launch your updated application.

7. Confirm that the update was a success.

8. Navigate back to chrome://extensions.

9. Click on the **Pack Extension** button.

10. Browse to the root of your Angular Chrome app.

11. Click on the **Pack Extension** button.

To recap the Local Chrome packing workflow, you navigated to Chrome's **Extensions** management page, installed the updates with a click, ensured that the updates are in order, and packed your updated Chrome app with a click. Now you are free to publish the update to the Chrome Web Store.

Deploying updates to the Chrome Web Store

Now that you've packaged your updated Angular Chrome app, it's time to delight your users by shipping them an update to the Chrome Web Store. Users that already have your app installed will receive the update automatically. #winning!

1. Locate your updated and packed Angular Chrome app.
2. Launch Google Chrome.
3. Navigate to `https://chrome.google.com/webstore/developer/dashboard`.
4. Authenticate with your Google account.
5. Locate your Angular Chrome app under the **Your Listings** header.
6. Select the **Edit** link at the right-hand side of the listing.
7. Select the **Load Updated Package** button.
8. Browse to your packed Angular Chrome app and upload.
9. Confirm that the update was a success.

Summary

Mastering your tool stack throughout all the phases of your development workflow, including postdeployment, is paramount in ensuring your users continue to engage with your application. You are the cornerstone in your tool stack responsible for holding everything else together. Without your regular use, development and updates of your application will slowly decay. Updates offer a means of adding more and more value to your application over time and provide a sense of safety as your competitors continue to innovate. The only way to protect your work from being disrupted is to continue disrupting it yourself through diligent innovation and craftsmanship.

8
Conclusion – AngularJS Deployment Essentials

"Made it."

– Quorra, Tron Legacy

We employed a number of tools that enhance your developer experience by amplifying your workflows to new heights. We further improved our tool stack by achieving single command deployments to Apache, Heroku, Firebase Hosting, as a Cordova mobile app, as a Chrome Cordova App, and as a Chrome Packaged App. Initial deployment is only as good as your postdeployment strategy, which is what you attained in the previous chapter. Harnessing the tools we covered in this text will allow you to deploy a single AngularJS application to new platforms and new customers. Achievement unlocked!

Developing a dynamic tool stack

I smile every time I deploy code with a single command. This feeling is pretty much how I measure my developer experience when working with any layer of my tool stack. This is the level I strove for when constructing the tool stack and workflow for each of the environments we covered.

It is inevitable that new, more radical, environments will grace us in the future and that is why your tool stack, at every layer, must remain dynamic. Maintain a watchful eye on your GitHub News Feed for new tools that improve your workflows. When you come across a repo that looks interesting, read the README file, and try it out. The speed of trial and error when testing these new tools is remarkably quick, making it easy to assess whether or not they'll improve your current tool stack and workflow. When you find the new hotness and it works for you, swap it in or add it to your stack. The community support on apps such as GitHub, Bower, and NPM seems to spawn new tools at an increasing rate.

Yet another way to further enhance your workflows and tool stacks is to create your own tools. Developers such as Pavel Feldman, Addy Osmani, Paul Irish, Chris Coyer, Bryan Ford, Sindre Sorhus, Umar Hansa, Ricardo Cabello, John Barton, Jan Keromnes, myself, and many more, all contributed to the modern web development workflow. In the summer of 2012, I had the distinct horror of participating in the Google Summer of Code program with the Eclipse Orion community. I proposed a new implementation of the Eclipse Orion web-based code editor as a Chrome DevTools extension that let developers edit their client-side code. We called the projects, Orion X, and it is still attracting daily installations from the Chrome Web Store. The best part of the experience was my mentor, a co-creator of FireBug and member of the Chrome team, John Barton. I learned a lot from John, and his other summer intern, Jan, about extending Chrome DevTools. Jan built an extension similar to mine, but instead used the CodeMirror web-based code editor for client-side code editing. The need and want for these tools brings developers such as John, Jan, and myself together into communities that continue to enhance our workflows.

You shouldn't feel like you have to care for your tools very much, beyond regular updates of course. Some tools have a ton of dependencies and while usually awesome, it can get fairly messy when they throw errors and slow down your development or deployment workflows. If this happens and the particular tool is not easily replaceable, you might not have a choice, but typically you'll be able to find another tool that provides overlapping functionality. On the deployment side, we covered a few ways to deploy to Apache, Heroku, and as a Cordova Mobile app. Knowing that these, at first, seemingly redundant tools exist might save you a lot of time or headaches when resolving a future issue. This is another reason to constantly improve your dynamic tool stack by trying new things. If you got a smidge too ambitious with your current tool selection and things stall in a bad way, you'll have your previous tool selection to fall back on. Also, if you ditched a tool for a previous choice, set a reminder in a month or two to try the tool out again or investigate the issue, fix it and submit a pull request. We're all moving at the speed of web and the tool will likely have improved.

Deploying early and deploying

This book is a proof that Angular is flexible enough to run amazingly well in a variety of environments with minimal changes or configuration. Angular's flexibility translates into environmental flexibility, affording itself many environments in which to run. Yet another facet of your developer experience is this ability to deploy your application in a multitude of different environments. I argue that a lack of flexibility in your chosen framework (specific environmental dependencies) is a negative developer experience because it limits your deployment possibilities. When choosing between frameworks, deployment flexibility should definitely be taken into consideration.

Thankfully, you made a solid choice by leveraging Angular, but beyond minimal to no environmental dependencies you should consider your options for rapid deployment. Rapid (or single command, as I've called it) deployment is a hallmark of an awesome developer experience when maintaining your production applications. Again, a lack of ability to rapidly deploy your code is a hallmark of a negative developer experience. If you come across an environment that you like for other reasons and there is not already a tool that facilitates single-command deployments, see if you can build one. If you do create an improved developer experience and its rad, consider open sourcing it to your community to gain some cool points with other members. Never settle; your tools can always improve and so can your experience.

Index

Symbol

.apk file
  signing 94

A

about view 26
account view 23
add-ons, Heroku 54
Analytics.addTrans() method 115
Analytics view
  using 64
Android Software Developer Kit
     (Android SDK)
  Android target, installing 79-81
  configuring 77
  emulator, creating 79-81
  installing 77
  OS X configuration 78
  URL 77
  Windows configuration 78, 79
Angular App, augmenting for Chrome
  about 101
  background.js file 103
  Chrome instance, deploying to 104
  Chrome Web Store, deploying 107
  deployment issues, troubleshooting 106
  manifest.json file 101
angular-google-analytics module
  about 114
  setting up 114, 115
  URL 115
AngularJS
  deployment feature 125

Angular web applications
  migrating, to hybrid mobile apps with
     Apache Cordova 81-83
  migrating, to hybrid mobile apps with
     Cordova Chrome app toolchain 89
  migrating, to hybrid mobile apps with
     PhoneGap Build 92
Apache
  configuring, for Angular applications 39
  PageSpeed Service 40, 41
  updates, deploying 116
Apache Cordova
  about 74, 75
  dependencies 76
  development environment, configuring 75
  installing 76
  used, for addressing issues 75
  used, for deploying app to physical
     device 87-89
  used, for migrating from Angular
     web applications to hybrid
     mobile apps 81-83
Apache HTTP server 29
application
  .apk file, signing 94
  code, moving into /www folder 85-87
  deploying, to emulator 83-85
  publishing 93, 94
  publishing, to Google Play Store 95
application hosting
  firebase-tools CLI, using 67

B

background.js file 103, 104
Batarang 15

Bower 13, 14

C

CCA
 used, for deploying updates to local
  emulator 119
 used, for deploying updates to physical
  device 120
chat view 20-22
Chrome
 Angular App, augmenting for 101
Chrome App
 about 97
 best type, selecting 98, 99
 need for 98
 policy, URL 102
 setup 100, 101
 updates, deploying to 121
 URL 99
Chrome instance
 deploying to 104, 105
Chrome Web Store
 deploying to 107-110
 updates, deploying to 122
 URL 107
command-line interface (CLI) 8, 76, 114
Content Delivery Network (CDN)
 about 70
 URL 70
Content Security Policy (CSP) 102
Cordova
 used, for deploying updates to local
  emulator 119
 used, for deploying updates to physical
  device 119
Cordova Chrome App toolchain
 development environment, configuring 90
 used, for migrating from Angular web
  applications to mobile apps 89
 used, for packaging Angular web
  applications for mobile apps 91
create, read, update, and delete (CRUD)
  method 57

D

Data view
 using 59, 60
deployment destination 30, 31
deployment issues
 troubleshooting 37, 95
 visual diff tool 38
 visual diff tool, using with Git 38
deployment issues, Chrome App
 troubleshooting 106
deployment issues, Firebase
 HTTP resources served, over HTTPS 70
 troubleshooting 69
deployment issues, Heroku
 troubleshooting 55
deployment, with GitHub
 automating 35-37
deployment, with SSH
 automating 35-37
development environment, for Apache
  Cordova
 configuring 75
development environment, for Cordova
  Chrome App toolchain
 configuring 90, 91
dynamic tool stack
 developing 124
dynos
 about 53
 features 53
 scalability 54

E

Eclipse Android Developer Tools (ADT)
 about 77
 options 77
Editor integration
 and Sublime Text 15
emulator
 app, deploying to 83-85
 app, deploying to physical device 87
Express
 about 49
 URL 49
express() method 52

U

updates
building, with PhoneGap Build 120
deploying, to Apache 116
deploying, to Chrome App 121
deploying, to Chrome Web Store 122
deploying, to Firebase Hosting 118
deploying, to Google Play Store 120
deploying, to Heroku 117
deploying, to local emulator with CCA 119
deploying, to local emulator with
    Cordova 119
deploying, to mobile apps 118
deploying, to physical device
    with CCA 120
packing, with local Chrome instance 121
updates, deploying to Apache
about 116
FTP client 116
FTP command-line interface 116
Git 117
SSH 117

V

version control
Git, using 8
GitHub, using 8
Virtual Private Server (VPS) 44
visual diff tool
about 38
using, with Git 38

W

web applications
tools 7, 8
web.js 52
workflow, Yeoman
about 10
Bower 13, 14
Grunt 12, 13
Yo 10, 11

X

Xcode
about 76
URL 75

Y

Yeoman 10
Yo 10, 11

Thank you for buying
AngularJS Deployment Essentials

About Packt Publishing

Packt, pronounced 'packed', published its first book, *Mastering phpMyAdmin for Effective MySQL Management*, in April 2004, and subsequently continued to specialize in publishing highly focused books on specific technologies and solutions.

Our books and publications share the experiences of your fellow IT professionals in adapting and customizing today's systems, applications, and frameworks. Our solution-based books give you the knowledge and power to customize the software and technologies you're using to get the job done. Packt books are more specific and less general than the IT books you have seen in the past. Our unique business model allows us to bring you more focused information, giving you more of what you need to know, and less of what you don't.

Packt is a modern yet unique publishing company that focuses on producing quality, cutting-edge books for communities of developers, administrators, and newbies alike. For more information, please visit our website at www.packtpub.com.

About Packt Open Source

In 2010, Packt launched two new brands, Packt Open Source and Packt Enterprise, in order to continue its focus on specialization. This book is part of the Packt Open Source brand, home to books published on software built around open source licenses, and offering information to anybody from advanced developers to budding web designers. The Open Source brand also runs Packt's Open Source Royalty Scheme, by which Packt gives a royalty to each open source project about whose software a book is sold.

Writing for Packt

We welcome all inquiries from people who are interested in authoring. Book proposals should be sent to author@packtpub.com. If your book idea is still at an early stage and you would like to discuss it first before writing a formal book proposal, then please contact us; one of our commissioning editors will get in touch with you.

We're not just looking for published authors; if you have strong technical skills but no writing experience, our experienced editors can help you develop a writing career, or simply get some additional reward for your expertise.

AngularJS Directives

ISBN: 978-1-78328-033-9   Paperback: 110 pages

Learn how to craft dynamic directives to fuel your single-page web applications using AngularJS

1. Learn how to build an AngularJS directive.

2. Create extendable modules for plug-and-play usability.

3. Build apps that react in real time to changes in your data model.

Mastering AngularJS Directives

ISBN: 978-1-78398-158-8   Paperback: 210 pages

Develop, maintain, and test production-ready directives for any AngularJS-based application

1. Explore the options available for creating directives, by reviewing detailed explanations and real-world examples.

2. Dissect the life cycle of a directive and understand why they are the base of the AngularJS framework.

3. Discover how to create structured, maintainable, and testable directives through a step-by-step, hands-on approach to AngularJS.

Please check **www.PacktPub.com** for information on our titles

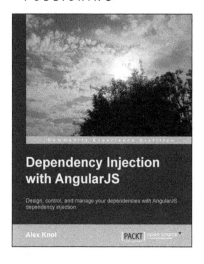

Dependency Injection with AngularJS

ISBN: 978-1-78216-656-6   Paperback: 78 pages

Design, control, and manage your dependencies with AngularJS dependency injection

1. Understand the concept of dependency injection.

2. Isolate units of code during testing JavaScript using Jasmine.

3. Create reusable components in AngularJS.

Learning AngularJS for .NET Developers

ISBN: 978-1-78398-660-6   Paperback: 202 pages

Build single-page web applications using frameworks that help you work efficiently and deliver great results

1. Implement complex frontend applications using AngularJS and rock solid web services using ServiceStack.

2. Become a more productive developer and learn to use frameworks that enforce good development practices.

3. Follow a gradual introduction to concepts with lots of examples and explore the evolution of a production-ready application.

Please check **www.PacktPub.com** for information on our titles